# Love That Heals

### God works in power at the London Healing Mission

## ANDY &
## AUDREY ARBUTHNOT

D1434142

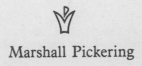

Marshall Pickering

Marshall Morgan and Scott
Marshall Pickering
3 Beggarwood Lane, Basingstoke, Hants RG23 7LP, UK

First published in 1986 by Marshall Morgan and Scott Publications Ltd
Part of the Marshall Pickering Holdings Group
A subsidiary of the Zondervan Corporation

**British Library CIP Data**

Arbuthnot, Andy
  Love that heals: God works in power at the London Healing
  Mission.
  1. Spiritual healing
  I. Title   II. Arbuthnot, Audrey
  615.8'52'0924   BT732.5

  ISBN 0-551-01337-0


Text Set in Plantin by Brian Robinson, North Marston, Bucks
Printed and bound in Great Britain by Hazell Watson & Viney Ltd,
Member of the BPCC Group, Aylesbury, Bucks.

# Contents

*All royalties from the sale of this book will be donated to the London Healing Mission, 20 Dawson Place, London, W2 4TL Tel: 01 229 3641.*

# Introduction

Little did I think, when at the age of eighteen I became an officer in the Scots Guards, that in due course I would be ordained and would be responsible for the work of the London Healing Mission. Still less did I foresee that, in the interim, I would go tea planting in the East, would stand for Parliament, and would finish up running one of the older Merchant Banks in the City of London! This book tells how the Lord has been leading my wife, Audrey, and me, in what has already been a rich and eventful life.

A story which Audrey and I have always enjoyed is of a man who had led a full life; there were parts of it when things had gone easily, and parts where, as with all of us, the going had been difficult. He died, and from the next world he looked back. He saw his life rather like a long sandy beach, and he could see his footsteps in the sand as he traced his way through each of the different stages of his life. He noticed that along much of that long beach there were two sets of footprints, and he realised the Lord had been with him. But he then saw that during those periods when the going had been particularly hard, there was only one set of footprints. He turned to Jesus, who was standing by him,

'Why, Lord,' he asked, 'did you abandon me when the going was tough?'

Jesus replied, 'Can you not see? When the going was difficult, there was only one set of footprints because I was carrying you.'

As Audrey and I look back on our own lives we realise how

wonderfully the Lord has been with us, both through sorrow and through joy.

The ministry into which He has led us is a joint ministry. Consequently, although this book has mainly been written by me, much thought has gone into it from us both. Chapter 4, on 'marriage' has mainly been written by Audrey.

Both our children have helped with writing this book with their comments and their encouragement. Our grateful thanks are due to them and to Jenny Arden-White who typed, and retyped the manuscript with unfailing cheerfulness. Since then she has married Charlie, our son, and so is now Jenny Arbuthnot.

As we minister, we are always conscious that the power to heal comes from the risen Lord and that in no way is it ours. Consequently, when recounting stories of people being healed, we have very often used the editorial 'we', so that no credit could be given to the person who was actually used as the vehicle for the Lord's healing.

Andy Arbuthnot

*London Healing Mission*
*20 Dawson Place*
*London W2 4TL*
*Telephone: 01-229 3641*

# 1

# Scots Guards

I remember clearly, some time in my teens, sitting back one day and wondering what life held for me. The war was still on and I had no real experience of peace time, having been only thirteen when the Second World War was declared, and I wondered what the future held. Of one thing I felt certain; I didn't want to live one day beyond the age of fifty. When one is in one's teens, anyone over fifty does seem pretty old! I remember feeling that over that age people often seemed senile, slow on the uptake, and altogether past it. I didn't believe that life could still be fulfilling and full of enjoyment. I didn't give a thought as to how death might come, but I remember being quite clear about that one thing: not one day, for me, please, beyond the age of fifty!

I look back with a quiet smile to those days, being now well into my sixtieth year. I find there is still the sense of looking forward to what is to come in life, and there may well be another twenty years of active life ahead. But this time there is the excitement of knowing that, for me, as a Christian, there will be even more fulfilment. There may well be suffering, but there will also be great joy. The ultimate future is assured. We can look forward, beyond death, to an eternity of joy, to being in the direct presence of the Lord, filled with delight beyond anything we can dream of, here in this world.

But as well as looking forward, at the age of sixty I can look back. And I look back over all that has happened in what has indeed already been a full life. It seems to me, now, that when I was a child the sun was always shining. I had a very happy home: mother, father and two older sisters, all of whom loved me; we lived in a large house in the country with a beautiful garden. It seems that the grass was always green, and the garden full of flowers.

Then, at the age of nine, I went away to boarding school, and a greyness seemed to come over my life. When I recollect those years, the weather seemed always to have been cloudy, and it was raining. I think the predominant memory of my school years is of a small boy who was always standing on the edge of a group of other boys. The other boys were laughing, joking, playing together, enjoying themselves and having fun; and one small boy was always on the outside of the circle, longing to join in, not knowing how to relate to the others, and suffering agonies of loneliness and self-consciousness. Although I enjoyed part of my school life, there was a lot of it that hurt.

Then, at the age of not quite eighteen, I joined up. This was the beginning of 1944 when, if one was conscripted, one might be sent into the forces or into the coal mines, and I wanted to get into the army. We had to volunteer if we were to be sure of that, so I volunteered for the Scots Guards, a regiment which all my uncles had been in. I joined up with others of my age a week before my eighteenth birthday on 7th January, 1944.

Drill, in particular, I found difficult, perhaps because I had overgrown my strength in my teens (I was all of six feet four inches). I found it hard to move as quickly, and as precisely, as was required on the parade ground at the Guards Depot at Caterham. But life was not without its lighthearted moments. There was what seemed an elderly Scots sergeant (looking back on it now, I doubt if he was as old as thirty). He had a kindly twinkle in his eye, and once when, as usual, I had executed some drill movement noticeably behind all the rest of the squad, he walked over the parade ground to me with these words:

'Arbuthnot, you look like a pregnant duck. Do you know what "pregnant" means?'

'Yes, sergeant,' I replied. I cannot remember the end of the conversation. Indeed I think the conversation ended rather abruptly at that point. But it was clear to me that he intended I should move a great deal quicker.

After thirteen weeks of training at the Guards' Depot, we moved on to Pirbright. That was more fun—there was more open-air work. We were out on the ranges practising shooting, or else in the lovely Surrey countryside doing little tactical exercises. After that followed four months at the OCTU at Mons Barracks, Aldershot. Once again, there was a certain amount of drill, and I remember the splendid Regimental Sergeant Major, a Coldstream Guardsman, who had a voice which would have shamed any bull chasing us mercilessly around the parade ground. Finally the great day came on 20th September, 1944, when we passed out, and for the first time we put on our officers' uniforms, complete with the single star of a Second Lieutenant. All of us were hoping to meet the Regimental Sergeant Major once we had been commissioned, as, strictly speaking, he would then have had to salute us. But he, being a man of great wisdom, took good care that he wasn't seen by us after the end of the passing-out parade.

Six months followed as a young officer back at Pirbright; then early in March 1945, a signal came through that Second Lieutenant Arbuthnot was to proceed overseas to join the Second Battalion of the Scots Guards, who were moving forward with the Guards Armoured Division, having crossed the Rhine, in the final phase of the war in Germany.

I remember that lovely spring morning, driving in a fifteen-hundredweight truck to the railway station at Brookwood. There was a cherry tree flowering, and the thought crossed my mind: was this the last spring that I would ever see? Would I ever see cherry trees flowering again? I didn't know at the time what the casualty rate was, although I knew that men were being wounded and killed pretty frequently. In fact, I subsequently learnt that the average length of life of a platoon commander in my battalion, even in those closing weeks of the war, was ten days.

The train took us up to London. We crossed London and

caught another train, with the usual Railway Warrant in place of a ticket, to take us down to Dover, and we boarded the cross-channel steamer just as dusk was falling. There were canvas hammocks for us to sleep in, one above the other, in tiers of four. As we steamed out of the harbour with lights dimmed, I walked right up to the bows of the ship. The sun was setting, it was getting dark and the ship began zig-zagging through the minefields which had been laid in the Straits of Dover. Again the thought came to me: this was not the first time that I was crossing the Channel from England to the Continent, but would it be the last? Nowadays, it seems curious to remember these thoughts, but I think my generation gained from being so close to death. Nowadays death is remote. It didn't do us any harm to realise that we were mortal, and that death might come at any moment.

I stood up there in the bows of the boat, as she ploughed her way, with no lights showing, towards the French coast, and I remember praying. I didn't know the Lord then, in the way that so many of us have come to know Him since, but I had an awareness of God. I had been to church every Sunday since I was five, and I had been confirmed. As I watched the foam spreading out from the bows of the ship, I prayed, 'God, I'm in your hands. It's up to you. I leave it to you as to whether I come back or not.' Then I turned and quietly went back to my bunk, the bottom of the four bunks in that tier.

About a week later, I caught up with my battalion. I was put to command what was known as Right Flank Platoon, in a Company commanded by a small man who seemed very fierce. Subsequently he became a Major General and indeed married a close friend of Audrey's and mine, and both of them are friends now. At that time he seemed a ball of energy, and I stood in awe of him. We were moving up fairly fast, transported in cumbersome three-ton lorries. The men sat behind on the wooden floorboards, bumping over the German roads, and, as the officer, I sat on a seat next to the driver, a seat that was only fractionally less uncomfy. One could see the appalling damage that had been done by allied bombers. I remember in particular one town, Julich, which was completely flat; there was not a single building standing as we drove through. Then we drove through Cologne. The cathedral was standing, but very little else; the destruction was appalling. And all the time there was the endless stream of refugees coming in the other direction, refugees from the East, fleeing before the Russian armies, realising that if they had to choose between the Russians, and the British, Americans or French, they were safer with people from the West. We didn't talk to them, we just saw them staggering along under heavy loads, carrying all they possessed, trudging wearily and heading to the West. We knew that every now and then they'd be rounded up and put in some crude camp for refugees, where at least they would have rest, and where they would be fed and watered. It was clearly a time of intense personal tragedy.

Fairly soon we were to take part in something of a set-piece attack. We had breakfast about half past six, on a lovely sunny morning in early summer. Then we moved forward and took up our positions, and early that afternoon, as we heard the crash of artillery fire from the tanks and self-propelled guns, for the first time I heard the crack and thump of live bullets being fired at us. We got down very quickly and lay on our stomachs in the open field where we were.

We had been used to the sound of bullets being fired over our heads during training, but now it was different. Now we knew that the men pressing the triggers meant those bullets to hit someone; might it be me? As we lay on the ground, there, taking shelter from the rifle and machine-gun fire, one of my platoon was just grazed by a bullet. I saw my platoon sergeant crawl over to him, and then sit up, bandaging his wound. The question which needed an immediate decision was this: was I going to lie there seeking shelter for myself whilst my platoon sergeant dressed the wound of one of my men? Or was I going to get up and help? I remember to this day the feeling as, gradually, I first sat up and then stood up, still hearing the bullets flying past and absolutely convinced that, any second, one would strike home and I would be in

13

the next world. But my platoon sergeant knew best. He knew that, although there was a lot of noise, the firing was sporadic; he knew there wasn't much to worry about. Having stood up I gained confidence, and walked over to join him. It was an experience shared by countless young men during the war and yet it was a very personal experience. However good the training had been, there was inevitably the feeling of being thrown in, for the first time, at the deep end.

Later that evening, we were advancing down a road and there was still a certain amount of rifle fire. I suddenly felt as if someone had thrown a brick at me very, very hard, and I found myself doing a ridiculous pirouette down the road, revolving slowly but out of control, round and round like a slow-spinning top. I remember one of the men saying to me in that lovely Scots accent, 'You've been hit, Sir.' I was slightly surprised, because there wasn't any pain. It felt very hot in my left side, but, as I subsequently discovered, it was only a flesh wound and nothing serious. I didn't really bother about it; the bullet had lodged in me only a quarter of an inch below the surface of the skin, and I limped slightly, but it didn't hurt. So the evening came and we bivouacked in the classic laager which we adopted in the Guards Armoured Division, the tanks drawn up in a circle facing outwards and the infantry inside the circle. My Company commander came up as I saw to my platoon and asked why I was limping. I said that there was a spot of blood but I didn't think it mattered. I was intensely frustrated when he ordered me—and 'ordered' was clearly the operative word—to go, myself, to the Regimental Aid Post. I suppose when I got there it was about half past seven. It shows how one can get carried away with the tension of what is happening, because it only occurred to me, then, when I was given some delicious stew to eat, that I hadn't eaten since breakfast that morning at half past six. I simply hadn't noticed being hungry.

As far as I was concerned that was the end of the war. I was flown back to Brussels—'walking wounded', was how they described us—and I spent the next few weeks in a military hospital. My only recollection of that time was my disappointment because I had kept the bullet in my pyjama pocket, and someone sent my pyjamas to the wash, so I lost it. A few weeks later, I went to a convalescent home on the Belgian coast. Then there was VE Day, with tremendous shouting and cheering as we learned that the war had finished in Europe. Then a few days leave at home, and back to join my battalion, which now was up in the neighbourhood of Bremen.

The next two and a half years were on the whole frustrating. I was already longing to get out of the army, to find some fresh purpose and to be free to lead my own life. We were to be demobilised by 'Age and Service' groups, and being still very young, my Age and Service Group wasn't due for demobilisation for quite a long while. But I was able to get myself posted to Vienna, where I had an uncle who was on the staff and who was able to apply for a young trainee Staff Lieutenant to join him.

I flew out to Vienna in a Dakota aircraft. It was very bumpy, and I remember well the disappointment as we came down through the clouds and saw a great broad river, which must have been the Danube, made famous by Strauss. But instead of being blue, it was dirty, grey-green and sluggish. I've always enjoyed Strauss's waltzes, but I think he must have been looking at life very favourably when he referred to the Danube as being blue.

The work was boring in the Control Commission for Austria to which I was attached. After all, I had had no experience of office life, so it was only natural that I should have been given humdrum jobs to do. But apart from the work there was a lot of fun. We were given a fortnight's leave every three months, and we got free travel passes to Styria and Carinthia in the British Zone of Austria. The country was lovely, the Wörthersee was unspoilt and one could stay in age-old inns for next to nothing. The people were simple and friendly.

But all the time I allowed myself to be eaten up by frustration and by the longing to get out of the army—to be free to find my feet and to be myself. Looking back on it, I wish so much that I had had some sound Christian teaching then. I wish that someone could have pointed out to me the words in the New Testament where Paul tells us that we are to give thanks in all things.[1] There was so much that I could have given thanks for, but instead I coveted what I hadn't got.[2] If only I could have been told that, for a Christian, the over-riding priority in life is his relationship with the Lord.[3] If only I could have learnt to have rested in peace with the Lord, and allowed Him to use that time in my life to develop a relationship with me. Furthermore, when eventually I was demobilised in October 1947, I might have had some idea of what life was about and what I wanted to do.

Although with many young people in Vienna there was a lot of fun, at the same time one was conscious the whole time of the tragedy of war. Vienna wasn't damaged to the same extent that some of the German cities were, but there had been some bombing, and the Russian army was much in evidence. I met a girl, whose husband had been a fighter pilot in the *Luftwaffe*, flying Messerschmitts. She heard he had been killed, and only days later three Russians broke into her flat, held a pistol to the head of her new-born son, and told her they would shoot him if she didn't allow each of them to rape her. She had no choice. With one old lady, who was a widow, a Russian soldier had tried to take off her gold wedding ring, but the finger joints were swollen with arthritis and it wouldn't come off. So he just cut her finger off in cold blood, and took the ring.

The Russians were primitive as well as cruel. When they first came to Vienna, most of the Russian soldiers had never seen a watch, and they would take the watches off any passer-by; you would see Russian soldiers going around with twelve or fifteen watches strapped on to their arms, right the way up from the wrist to the elbow. They were fascinated by the sight of the hands going round, and they learnt to wind the watches to keep the hands moving.

Imprinted on my mind is the tragedy of the stations on the Stadtbahn, the underground railway of Vienna. The stations were plastered with pathetic notices, each with a photograph,

16

and each notice saying: 'Has anyone heard of my husband, named so-and-so, last heard of on the Eastern Front?' and then the date of the last letter that had come through from that ghastly carnage when the Russians were destroying the German armies. I doubt if many of them ever heard of their relatives again.

Our office was the Schönbrunn Palace, built in luxury in the middle of the eighteenth century, and beautifully decorated in baroque and rococo. It had been the summer residence of the Emperors, and it seemed so sad that it should be spoilt by being used as offices by the Control Commission for Austria. It seemed terrible too, as we saw the Viennese char-ladies scrubbing—yes, scrubbing—what had been exquisite parquet floors, but which were now being ruined as they were cleaned. I remember the first office that I worked in, in the Secretariat; it had been Maria Theresia's bedroom, a lovely room with crimson damask coverings on the walls and beautiful tapestries.

Shortly before I arrived, the Commander-in-chief had given a ball in the State ballroom; it must have been the most lovely occasion and I always regretted having missed it. All the chandeliers, and some of them were about nine feet across, had been lit with candles. The cut glass was exquisite, and the flickering candlelight, refracted into different colours by the prisms of the cut glass, must have been very beautiful. Furthermore, I don't know what it was, but a Viennese waltz played by a Viennese string band was different from the same waltz played anywhere else. Somehow, they've got it in their blood. I remember, to this day, watching a couple waltzing on a frozen pool with just a single Viennese violinist playing; it was one of the loveliest things I have ever seen.

Even at the height of the Austro-Hungarian Empire, the public had been able to walk all through the grounds of Schönbrunn Palace, right up to the palace windows. The only part they had not been allowed to walk in, was the small private garden of the Emperor. I remember being impressed at such a degree of democracy in the Imperial heyday.

Other things took us back to earlier years. For example the

lawns were immaculately kept, and I remember my amazement when I saw them being scythed by old men; no lawnmower was allowed on those lawns. The scythes had long, narrow blades, and, knowing how hard it is to be effective with a scythe, even with something which has stiff stems like nettles, one realised how razor-sharp those blades must have been, and how skilled the old men were who wielded them, for them to be able to cut the soft stems of grass on the lawns so meticulously.

## 2

# Tea Planting in the East

Eventually I was demobilised at York in October 1947. As I came down in the train, wearing an army-issue, grey pin-striped civilian suit, which bulged in all the wrong places, and with army-issue cuff-links keeping my army-issue shirt cuffs in order, I realised that I hadn't the faintest idea what life was about or what I wanted to do with it. I had had my first girl friend in Vienna, and had been unable to handle the relationship, and I still hadn't learnt to stand on my own feet.

On 5th August, 1948, I joined Arbuthnot Latham & Co Ltd, a firm which had been founded a hundred and fifteen years earlier by my great-great uncle John Alves Arbuthnot, together with his partner, Alfred Latham. I remember walking in at the door, that morning, with my father, and wondering how long I'd stay at this new job and what it would lead to. Little did I know that I would work there for nearly thirty-five years. Still less did I foresee the changes and developments which would take place during that period.

The total staff numbered twenty-seven, which included the five Directors. The total revenue of the firm, before paying any salaries or overheads, was about one hundred thousand pounds. Most of this was earned from commission on selling tea from various tea estates which we ran in what is now called Sri Lanka, but was then known as Ceylon. Although we called ourselves Merchant Bankers, and indeed were accepted as such by the Bank of England, our total revenue from banking, again before paying any overheads, was a mere five thousand pounds a year.

A year later, I was sent out to Ceylon to learn something about tea planting. We were responsible to the shareholders of several public companies for looking after their tea estates, so we needed to know what was involved. I went out by sea on the latest ship of the P and O Line, the SS *Himalaya*, which did the journey to Colombo in the then extraordinarily fast time of seventeen days.

The voyage was fun. I remember calling at Gibraltar. We were able to land there for a few hours, and we climbed over the Rock, that great mass of stone rising sheer out of the Mediterranean Sea. Then a day or two later we passed Malta, clearly visible in the early morning sun. Then came Port Said, and as we were anchored there before starting to go through the Canal, I recall looking over the side of the ship and seeing how beautifully clear the water was. We took it in turns to throw coins into the sea, and watched as little native boys duck-dived down into the depths, swimming literally like fish until they caught up with the falling coins and put them into their mouths. Then they would come up and break surface again, and before long their cheeks were bulging with coins as they grinned and watched for the next coin to be thrown. Eventually we sailed slowly through the Suez Canal, so narrow a waterway that you felt almost as though you were going on land yourself. We finally came out through the Canal at the other end, into the blistering heat of the Red Sea, with the heat reflected back from the hills and the sand on either side. Then on past Aden, to Bombay, where for the first time I saw a snake charmer. A small, ancient Indian sat cross-legged on the pavement, playing on a simple flute whilst a cobra in a basket swayed rhythmically before him. Some of them had been de-fanged; one never knew whether they were dangerous or not. In Bombay we swam in a lovely swimming pool called Breach Candy. This was an irregularly shaped pool, fringed with palm trees, and you realised you were in the tropics. Then we steamed on, down the western coast of India, until one night we were told that the following morning we would be landing in Colombo. I remember going up on deck in my dressing gown, and seeing the sun rising at six o'clock in the morning over the jungle to the east; there we were, moored in the harbour in Colombo. Two of the partners from George Steuart and Co, our agents in Colombo, came out to meet me, and somehow I knew, as they took me back in their launch to the shore, that I was going to enjoy my time in Ceylon.

I was met by George and Betty Spedding, a delightful couple in their thirties, who drove me up to Rookwood Estate, where I was to spend the next six months learning about tea planting.

Under George's pretty close supervision, I was put in charge of No. 2 Division on the estate, a division of some three hundred acres, and with some three hundred coolies, as we used to call them, working there. Shortly before I arrived, Ceylon had become an independent dominion, and already we were having to get used to referring to them as 'labourers'.

The country was lovely. The bungalow was about five thousand feet up in the hills and wherever you looked there was a sheet of tea bushes of unbroken green. At fifty-yard intervals throughout the tea there were shade trees, for tea, being a jungle plant, doesn't like too much sun. As one looked over the hillsides, here and there a gang of labourers were plucking the tea. Mostly they were women. They had big baskets hanging down their backs secured by leather thongs over their foreheads, and as they plucked with both hands they would throw the leaves back over their shoulders into the baskets. The men were mostly employed with the heavier work, replanting, digging-in manure, lopping the shade trees when their growth became too prolific and making roads.

It was a wonderful experience for a young man. Before I went out I had always wondered at the back of my mind whether, if you went to a different part of the world, with a totally different culture, the people, themselves, would be fundamentally different. But I saw that this was not so. The culture could not have been more different from that in which I had been brought up. These were simple men and women, living a simple existence, a whole family living in a single room, earning their living from the soil, most of them unable to read or write, and all of them either Buddhists or Hindus. But one learnt very quickly that beneath the different-coloured skin, and despite the different cultural veneer, they were the same sort of men and women that I had known already in my life. They reacted the same way. They loved the same way. They had the same spites and jealousies, and I realised that mankind is basically the same the world over.

Living among people who were leading such simple lives, one saw something of what we in the West have lost. Often three generations would be living in the same room. By day, father and mother would be out, working in the tea, and one would see how the grandchildren and the grandmother bene-fitted from each other's company. Often as I meet some grandmother today, living a lonely life with little purpose, and longing for the love of relatives around her, I think how much happier those grandparents were on the tea planta-tions. They had no television and no radio, they couldn't read or write, and they had no newspapers, but they lived among their relatives and their friends. They were never lonely, they didn't have to work, and they could go and sit on the terraces of the coolie lines whenever they wanted to. Around them the children were playing. They helped the children, they brought them up and they had a purpose in life. They belonged. There is such desperate loneliness in the artificial culture that we live in, today.

One of the first things I asked was the Tamil for 'thank you'. I was surprised when I was told that there was no such word. The reasoning goes like this. If I do something to help you, I'm only doing it, so they believe, to acquire merit for myself in heaven; so why on earth should you bother to thank me if I'm doing something for my own good! Then I asked about the spirits whom they worshipped. As we drove at night through the native villages, almost every hut had a little platform on a stilt in its bit of garden, and on that platform there would be offerings, some coconut oil or a little ghee (native butter). I remember asking who these spirits were. I was told that it was always the bad spirits to whom they made offerings. They argued: 'We believe in good spirits and we believe in bad spirits. But the good spirits are all right; they won't hurt you. Therefore why bother with them! It's the bad spirits we need to placate; it is therefore the bad spirits to whom we make our offerings!'

Ceylon is a beautiful island—two thousand years ago the Romans called it 'The Pearl of the East'. But there was suffering too. On the whole the people had enough to eat, but we saw a lot of animals suffering. Invariably, when one saw a native cart, drawn by a little underfed cow, the driver would be sitting on the shafts kicking with his naked foot where it would hurt most, to get her to hurry along. Then one remembered the philosophy of the East; if I see you suffering, I know that it is because in a former incarnation you have sinned. It is therefore your fate that you should suffer now. So why should I interfere with your fate? Why should I lift a finger to relieve your suffering? How anyone, in the light of this, can claim that all the world's major religions are of equal value, is beyond me.

I don't believe that any of us can realise what we in Western Europe owe to centuries of Christian culture and religion, unless we have lived for a time in a country that has not had that background. Much as I loved Ceylon, I should call it Sri Lanka now, I couldn't help being aware, in so many ways, of the fact that they had not got centuries of Christian culture behind them. In England, and in Western Europe, there are certain standards of kindness, decency and uprightness which still today we look for in each other, but out there one couldn't help realising the absence of those standards. You may retort that England is no longer Christian, and there is a real sense in which that is true. But the fact remains that so much of our thinking is derived from former generations who accepted Christian standards.

We didn't see much wild life in Ceylon. Everywhere there were buffaloes, but these were domesticated buffaloes, kept like cattle by the natives, shambling along with their heads hung low and with their great horns curving outwards and backwards from their foreheads. There was a patch of jungle around the bungalow, not more than a few acres, and I remember the Speddings were always careful about their dachshunds, because a leopard lived there from time to time, and leopards like small dogs. But we never saw him. There were snakes; you saw the occasional rattle snake; occasionally, very occasionally, you even saw a cobra, and I think I once saw a tic polonga. I forget which of these snakes, the cobra or the tic, this applies to, but both are lethal, and one brings death because when it has bitten a man his blood coagulates and circulation ceases. Earlier in this century, life was primitive for the tea planters, and the old remedy for a snake bite was simple. A man would be given a bottle of neat whisky, which would thin the blood and help reduce the risk of coagulation, and then, in relays, his friends would take him, two at a time, one by each arm, and keep him walking for twenty-four hours to keep the blood moving. It was said that usually you survived—that is, if you could survive the treatment.

Perhaps in some ways the most fascinating side of Ceylon life centred around the old civilisation, of some fifteen hundred to two thousand years ago. There had been a great kingdom in Ceylon. It was based on an intricate irrigation system, a system of tanks or reservoirs. In each case the water in some river had been penned in behind a great earthen bank or bund, perhaps twenty feet thick. Then, as the water was allowed to flow down, controlled by sluices, it watered the paddy fields below, where they were growing rice; thence it might flow into yet another tank or reservoir and the process was repeated.

The natural skill of those early peoples was considerable. I remember reading that, earlier this century, engineers had wanted to bring back into use a bund that had been damaged centuries before. They repaired this great earth work, but they needed, as every engineer will know, to put sluices in the mile-long earthen wall of the dam. With all the advantage of modern scientific knowledge, they calculated precisely

24

where, in that long dam, the sluices should go. As they dug into the soil, they found within a foot or two, the ancient sluices built there by men who had worked by the light of nature, some fifteen hundred or more years earlier. What was more, as they dug out those early sluices, they found that the men of those days had known what the modern engineer knows, that the sides of a sluice in a dam should not be parallel, but should be sloping.

Between the wars, men discovered some of the cities of that civilisation, cities which had been grown over by the jungle, and which it fell to twentieth century man to clear again. I remember seeing a statue of a reclining Buddha, perhaps thirty feet long, hewn out of the living rock in one of these cities, Polonnaruwa. Then there was Sigiriya, an enormous rock with a top extending to some three-quarters of an acre, rising a hundred feet sheer out of the flat, jungle-covered country. The top of it had been used as his fortress, by some earlier king who had ruled in that part of Ceylon, and there was only one way up. As you went up the side of the rock, you passed quite beautiful frescoes of dancing girls, executed many centuries earlier. You then went on and saw where the swarms of wild bees had had their nests, before they were cleared away for the benefit of tourists. Finally you came to the top.

The story is told that at the beginning of this century, a Royal princess, one of Queen Victoria's daughters, paid a visit to Ceylon with great ceremony. She was taken, with all her entourage, the ADCs, ladies-in-waiting and the royal party, to see the sights of Sigiriya, and those watching from afar looked on as the party slowly ascended the path winding up the face of this great rock. Then, as they watched, they saw with horror, as one of Her Royal Highness's ADCs bent down, seized the hem of Her Royal Highness's billowing skirts, and proceeded to raise her skirts above Her Royal Highness's head, thus exposing all the royal underwear to full view. Little did they know what had happened. Some of the bees had not been cleared, they had attacked the royal princess, and the ADC, with complete disregard for his personal safety, was holding the Princess's skirts above her head to protect her. Those bees are dangerous. It is said that seven stings are equivalent to one cobra bite. I don't know what happened to the ADC, but I trust that he was suitably rewarded for his selfless loyalty to his Monarch's daughter.

We sometimes went to visit one of those tanks from that earlier civilisation. Many of them were large, perhaps twenty acres or more. I once took out a native catamaran on one. This was a dug-out canoe, simply a tree trunk hollowed out and with a rough seat put across the middle; because of the weight of the trunk it lay low in the water. An out-rigger, something similar to the canoe itself only much smaller, floated about five feet out from the canoe and parallel with it, secured by two rough struts. I remember going out at sunset and paddling rather further than I had meant to. People said that there had been crocodiles in that tank, but as sometimes happens, the crocodiles for no apparent reason had migrated; they said there were no crocodiles there now. I paddled to the other end and watched the birds as they swooped down from their perches to feed off the fish; then as I started back to the rest-house where I was staying, the light started to fade. Dark falls quickly in the tropics, and I was caught out in the half light, alone in the catamaran, sitting only a few inches above the level of the water. There was a slight wind and a ripple on the surface of the water. As I looked behind me, and saw the ripples, time after time I kept wondering whether, when the natives said that the crocodiles had migrated, perhaps they hadn't counted right, perhaps one crocodile had stayed behind; was I sure I wasn't seeing the snout of a crocodile swimming towards me, with the rest of him submerged beneath the water? I paddled as fast as I could get that dug-out canoe to go, until I landed it with a sigh of relief by the rest-house.

George Spedding had a nice story about crocodiles. When he was young, he told how he had stayed out too late at a party, and I think had drunk more than was good for him; he was travelling back on his motorbike along the narrow bund of one of these tanks. And George, being George, and having had too much to drink, was travelling too fast. Too late, in the dim lights of a pre-war motorbike, he saw a whole family of crocodiles lying right across the bund, enjoying the warm soil, warmed by the sun of the preceding day. George had the presence of mind to do the only sensible thing under the circumstances. He couldn't stop in time, so he opened his throttle, stood up and rode his motorbike, bump-bump-bump, over the backs of the reclining crocodiles.

Some people used to shoot wild game in Ceylon. There were those who still hunted buck with deer hounds, on foot, and that must have been very close to primitive man hunting his prey. One man I knew out in Ceylon—Smithy, we called him—had lost an eye because he had been hunting buck with a pack of hounds before the war. The buck had stood at bay, and he had gone in with a knife in his hands to finish it off; the buck had caught him in the eye with one of its antlers, and he had returned with one eye the less. That was a fairer kind of hunting than people indulge in nowadays.

Then after a year, back I came, this time on one of the Orient Line liners, the *Orcades*. I landed at Tilbury, and within a few days I was at work again in the office, working once more as a clerk. I remember very clearly the frustration of being back in City life after the freedom of working on the tea estate in the East.

# 3

# *Audrey and the Children*

One of my memories is of sitting in my little bed-sitting room, at the top of a house in London, the room being only just big enough to take a bed, a small arm-chair, some sort of a cupboard and a single gas ring. I remember looking out over the roofs of the neighbouring houses, and being aware that somehow I was poised above an abyss. I just knew that somehow, spiritually speaking, I had to hang on to whatever I had got, which wasn't much—anything rather than letting go and just sinking into the abyss below.

I wasn't long out of the army, and I had no idea of any purpose for my life. My father kept saying to me, 'What do you want to do with your life?' and I simply didn't know the answer to that question. Looking back, I wish so much that there had been some Christian person who could have told me that I would never find the answer to that question, because, quite simply, it was the wrong question. If only I had had somebody who could have shown me that I needed to put God—God, as revealed in Jesus—absolutely first and foremost in my life,[4] that I needed to allow Him to have His way with me, to allow Him to reveal Himself to me, and that then, in His own perfect timing, He would guide me in the next step.[5] The trouble with eternally asking yourself, 'What do I want to make of my life?', is that each time you ask it, you are looking inwards. If only I had had a mature Christian to help me to turn outwards to the Lord, then in time it would have been possible for Him to have filled me with His peace, and with that peace would have come the still, quiet voice of certain assurance, and knowledge of His Will.

There is so much in that lovely story of Elijah, when he was afraid and was seeking the Lord.[6] In a way he had the same problem as I had: what was to come next? We read in that early account, from nearly three thousand years ago, how there came a great wind; one can imagine the gale tearing up the valley, blowing branches off the trees, and Elijah shivering against the back wall of his cave. But he knew that in that great wind there was not the voice of God. Then came an earthquake and in that hilly country, it must have seemed that the hills themselves were being shaken to their foundations. Elijah must have been aware of the tremendous, earth-shaking power which caused those convulsions, and yet he knew within himself that the voice of God was not in that power. Then followed the fire—and it is interesting that in nature, the sequence is often as the prophet described it, first a strong wind, then an earthquake, and then a fire. The fire would have torn up the valley, burning all that was before it. Elijah shrank still further against the back of the cave, and he knew that in that fire there was not the voice of God. Then we read that when all was silent, he came forward and moved out on to the little bit of open ground in front of the cave. In the silence, he heard a still, small voice, and he knew that *that* was the voice of God.[7]

I wish so much, now, that I could have stopped thrashing around and going over and over the question, 'What do I want to do with my life?' I needed to put the Lord first, and to remember those words in the Old Testament, 'I am a jealous God,[8] and you will have no other gods before Me.' I wish I could have realised that I was making a little tin-pot god out of my seeking. If only I could have followed Jesus, when He said the first and great commandment, coming above everything else, is to love the Lord our God with everything we've got.[9] Then as I experienced His peace I would have come to hear that still, small voice of certainty.

Of one thing however I was certain, and it seemed to me so obvious, that it never dawned on me that it was from God: I must not leave my job in the City until I knew for sure what

I wanted to do next. I knew I disliked the job, I found it boring, and at that stage, I got no fulfilment out of it. But it seemed to me self-evident that I must stay there just as long as it took for me to be sure what I was to do next. Little did I know then, that this would only come in prayer in the autumn of 1981! So I stayed on in the City for no better reason than that I couldn't be sure of what to do next. Looking back, I can discern the hand of the Lord so clearly. Sometimes, it is hard to see the Lord's hand at work in one's life, at the time; often, it is only years later that one realises how He has been leading.

Meanwhile, as I sat in my little bed-sitting room under the roof, my mind turned to marriage. I remembered that at school I had thought about marriage, and I had written it off. I was well aware that I simply didn't know how to relate to boys of my own age. How much harder would it be to relate to a girl! I knew no girls. How could I ever relate to one! And if my recollection of school was largely of standing, lonely and self-conscious, outside a group of boys who were all friends together, how would I ever become friends with a girl, let alone reaching the degree of intimacy which I sensed was needed before one got married?

However, three years later, early in July 1951, I was working in the office in the City when a friend rang up and asked me to go to watch the tennis at Wimbledon that afternoon. I refused. I'd had a couple of days off the previous month, and I simply hadn't got the face, family firm or no family firm, to ask for another. But the friend insisted. They needed one more man to make up the party. They had got the ticket for Wimbledon. Would I join them? Eventually, I said that I would at least ask one of the Directors, but I said I expected the answer, 'No'. I remember so well asking him, and the kindly expression on his face as he said, 'Why not? Take the afternoon off and go and enjoy yourself at Wimbledon.' So I went along to have lunch with the party of six or eight young people who were gathering in my friend's house in Sprimont Place, in Chelsea. A girl walked into the room with a white coolie hat. I don't think we talked during

30

lunch, but David, our host, divided us up after lunch, because the seats weren't all together—they were all for the Centre Court, but they were mostly in odd pairs—and this girl sat next to me. I remember well asking her telephone number as I left. Thirteen months later, Audrey and I were married.

She was an only child, and like all only children she had found herself with much time to reflect. She told me that she had been much impressed by an experience of her father's in the first war. He had had to take a message through Arras, up to the front line, whilst Arras was being heavily shelled. He wasn't an especially religious man, but he was a Christian. As he approached Arras on his motorbike, and saw the shells falling heavily upon the town, he prayed to the Lord and committed himself to Him. Then, as he started to enter the town, the shelling lifted. I don't know if there was any speed limit, but he certainly didn't observe one. He opened his throttle to the full, and was out of Arras as quickly as he could get through. But he used to relate how almost as soon as he was clear of Arras, on the other side, the shelling started up again. He then went on, up to the front line, delivered his message, and set out on the return journey which again was to take him through Arras. Exactly the same thing happened. As he approached Arras on his return journey, he prayed, and the shelling lifted just for the time that it took him to ride his motorcycle at breakneck speed through the battered town. Audrey grew up with this story as a child, and, looking back on it, she realises now that it was the beginning of her trust in God.

At the age of eleven she was sent to boarding school which she thoroughly enjoyed. Her religious conviction grew stronger. In other ways she was quite a handful. Indeed, one term her parents had to threaten to stop her riding, which was her great love, unless she would conform more to the school rules. I gather this was the only threat which they thought could have achieved the desired result.

Then came the Second World War, and the experience which countless other people had, of going down each night

31

into the air-raid shelter. She subsequently wrote:

> We were always locking ourselves out of the house by mistake, and getting fed up with being down in the shelter. I remember then making a promise to the Lord, as so many of us do. I said, "Lord, if only you will see us all through this war, then I promise that I will always follow you and do what you want."

> How many of us do that, and how many of us really intend it at the time—and then, when things are all right, we forget about God! It's strange how we always run to God in times of trouble, and then when things are going all right, we forget Him. But our Lord wants us, doesn't He, to be thinking about Him all the time, and to concentrate on Him and to live our lives with Him, not just in times of danger, but in times of happiness, too. He never leaves us. He tells us, doesn't He, that He will never, never forsake us;[10] it's only we that turn our backs on Him. He is always there whenever we turn to Him.

Although it was not till many years later that we each entered into that deep personal relationship of love with the Lord which forms the heart of the Christian faith, we had both been brought up to believe in God. For my part I knew I couldn't marry someone who did not believe in Him. Audrey always remembers that before I asked her to marry me, I asked her if she believed in God. To my relief she said 'Yes' to both questions.

Our wedding was on 9th August, 1952. We were married at Stedham, a little village near Audrey's home, and in the church which many years earlier her great grandparents had rescued from dilapidation, and restored. Audrey's mother provided us with a profusion of brilliant gladioli, and we spent most of the day before our wedding decorating the church ourselves.

We set off for the continent for our honeymoon, and it must have been one of the very rare occasions when three people went off on a honeymoon! Those were the days of foreign currency shortage, and tourists who went abroad were limited to a very small amount of foreign currency. We had a friend, however, who was an Australian, and Australians were not limited. We arranged, therefore, to take him with us across the Channel, on the first day of our honeymoon, so that he could cash his travellers cheques in France, and provide us with the extra foreign currency we needed. We would then repay him in Sterling, on our return to England. I remember the boat was late arriving in Dieppe, because of rough seas, and the road from Dieppe to Paris in those days was poor. We were extremely keen—for reasons which can be appreciated—that he should not miss his aeroplane back from Paris to London that evening, and we drove at breakneck speed, in our very old car, down this bumpy road to the French capital. He was very long suffering, I remember, because there wasn't even time to give him dinner. We helped him cash his cheques and then pushed him onto the aeroplane. However we were eternally grateful to him for his help.

The car was a pre-war Rover, which we had bought for £75. The trouble was that it kept stopping. It even broke down in Brighton before we got across the Channel. I'd had some training in the internal combustion engine when I was in the army, and each time that it stopped, I duly opened the bonnet, and either cleaned the plugs, or made some other adjustment to the engine. I was mildly pleased that after ten minutes or so, spent fiddling under the bonnet, it invariably started up again, and I think, at that stage of our married life, Audrey formed the impression that she had married someone who was really quite mechanically-minded. It was only towards the end of the honeymoon, however, during that hot August of 1952, that we realised that the pipe which took the petrol from the tank to the carburettor, passed quite close to the cylinder block, and in the heat, the petrol was vaporising before it got to the carburettor. Consequently, all that was needed for the car to go again, was to let it cool down for ten minutes or so, upon which the petrol would cease to vaporise, and all would be well.

That Audrey ever married me was something of a miracle. I can only say, deeply and sincerely, thank God that she did. Looking back, although I was by now twenty-six, I was too immature emotionally for a stable relationship, too immature to contemplate matrimony, and too immature to think of being a father. But she married me, she stuck by me, and we both thank God continually for the wonderful relationship that has developed, and for the love that the Lord has given each of us, for the other. I remember, quite clearly, after we had been married for a few months, the two of us agreeing that in marriage one has all the advantage of being alone, but without the loneliness. Subsequently He blessed us with two lovely children.

When we were first married, I moved into Audrey's flat which was on the top floor of a very rickety house, just north of Notting Hill Gate. We were advised by an architect friend that we would be unwise to have more than eight people in the house at any one time, lest the floor gave way. We were a little concerned, therefore, when all the family came to stay for the Coronation! A month or two later, Audrey did go through the floor, but luckily not too far. After a few months, we decided to move to Chelsea, and eventually took a large ground floor flat, near the river. Audrey was splendid, because for the three years we were in that flat, we let three self-contained bed-sitting-rooms. When we married, I had no money, and my bank account was in the red. The income from those rooms helped to put us on our feet financially.

Our first child, Caroline, was born while we were in that London flat. Audrey had her in Queen Charlotte's hospital, which is a lovely place. It is solely for maternity cases; consequently it is only exceptionally that somebody goes there who is ill. Perhaps this is partly responsible for the happy atmosphere. In those days, hospitals were not as enlightened as they are now, when husbands can be with their wives during the whole course of labour. I would have loved to have been, and I felt sad that I wasn't allowed to be with her when she went into the delivery theatre. But all the previous twenty-four hours, whilst the labour pains were gradually getting stronger, I was able to be with her, and it was a joy to be able to rub her in the small of her back and make it easier for her. Perhaps, also, because I had been with her so much, I remember there was not the slightest anxiety in my mind when the delivery became imminent, and she was wheeled away.

We have always enjoyed sharing things together, and since Caroline, our daughter, was soon feeding from a bottle, I remember I used to take turns with the early morning feeds. It was a lovely summer, the summer of 1954, but however lovely the early morning, I got tired of seeing the sun rising at half past four or five, above the roofs of Chelsea.

Soon after Caroline's birth, both of us having been brought up in the country, we decided it would be nice to move out of London. After much searching, we found a lovely little house in the village of Tilford, near Farnham in Surrey, and we made our home there for the next eight years. A year later, in June, 1956, our second child was born, a son. I remember there was much discussion about what he should be named. My clear recollection was that we chose Caroline's name not merely before we were married, but before we were engaged—although Audrey does not, I think, agree with my recollection. But—and again I think she might disagree with my memory—I remember clearly Audrey having serious doubts as to whether we should call our son Charles, 'because', she said, 'inevitably, everybody will call him Charlie.' However, Charles he was, and he was duly christened in the village church. I found it quite amusing that the first person, then, who changed to calling him 'Charlie', was Audrey herself.

Looking back on it, I think we both regret not having had two more children. Yet the reason we didn't was because we were cautious about the money situation. When our children were small, Arbuthnot Latham was still small. The Directors' fees had always been £2000 a year, and it was a long time before anybody had the idea of increasing them. We were determined to give our children the best education, and so we limited our family to two. But we did find that, having a small family, we were very close to each other.

When the children were small, Audrey remembers how one afternoon she realised they were both hiding in a cupboard. Much excited whispering came from behind the cupboard door. She asked what they were doing. 'We're

35

playing at being God', came the reply. 'We're here but you can't see us.' The years went by, gradually the children matured and grew older, and the sad day came when first one and then the other went away to boarding school. Audrey found it particularly hard to adjust to them being away for much of the year, and we both hated saying goodbye to them at the end of the holidays.

In her teens, Caroline's main love was riding. We resisted buying a pony for her until we both felt fairly sure that her desire for a pony was not just a passing whim. Then for the next five or six years, we had a succession of ponies. We were very fortunate in that a friend, who lived next door, was a rider of almost Olympic standard; she enjoyed teaching children and she taught Caroline. But although Caroline became an accomplished rider, she never really had the desire to get to the top. I well remember her coming back one day from riding on the common, on her first pony. We asked whether she had put him over the small jumps in the field. 'No', Caroline replied, 'He didn't seem to want to, and I wanted him to enjoy the ride too.'

Charlie went away in due course to his Prep School, which was fairly tough, but which he survived well. But he didn't excel in any of the games they played there, whether cricket, football or rugby. Then the day came when he went on to his next school. We sent him to Eton, where I had been, and both my father and my grandfather before me. We have always been a rowing family, and it seemed natural for Charlie to take to the river. I remember going out in a sculling boat, and watching him in his little boat, his first summer at Eton. Afterwards, I commented rather sadly to Audrey that I didn't think he would ever be any good at rowing either. How wrong I was to be proved!

Two or three summers passed, and Charlie's rowing really began to take off. I shall always remember what was, for all of us, an intensely exciting summer, when Charlie was sixteen. Charlie was judged not good enough to row for Eton, but he stroked the Second Eight, and they won one race after another. Half of them went in for the Junior National

Championships at Nottingham as a 'Four', and although none of them was over sixteen, they won. It was then decided by the selectors, that this four should represent Great Britain in the Junior World Championships with Charlie rowing at stroke. The following year, Charlie stroked the Eton Eight, and again they were chosen to represent Great Britain in the Championships. We went out to Ratzeburg, in Western Germany, where the Championships were being held, and we watched as Charlie's Eight—or perhaps I should say the Great Britain Eight—came in sixth. The visit to Ratzeburg was the first time that I had ever actually seen the 'Iron Curtain', which seals off Communist Europe from the free West. It certainly looked formidable, with machine guns in the watch towers, and the impenetrable barbed wire fence stretching as far as the eye could see.

Talking to other parents one knows that in many families, the children start going off on their own holidays in their early teens. We were fortunate, in that the children always wanted to come with us until well into their late teens, and we had many happy holidays together. The last holiday was in Scotland. A couple of months before, Charlie had remarked, one evening, 'Why don't we walk across Scotland this summer?' I think I had brought some office work back with me that evening, and without thinking what I was saying, I said, 'OK, let's'. I realised, subsequently, that the die had been cast. Anyhow, we duly hired a caravan, Audrey stocked it up with provisions, and we drove it up to the West coast of Scotland. The plan was that two or three of us should walk, whilst the remaining one or two of us would drive the car and caravan and pick up the walkers at the next stage. When four of you, including two grown-up children, are living in a small caravan, you get to know each other pretty well. There was no question of either Audrey or me getting up, until we had folded up the beds, because there simply wasn't the floor space to get out of bed and stand on. I well remember, too, when Audrey made the very bold suggestion of heating something in the little oven, that Caroline expostulated, 'You can't do that, Mum, the oven is the only place I've got for my clean clothes!' Mercifully the weather was fine, and it was a lovely last holiday that the four of us had together.

Caroline went on to University, and spent some time working with the Cyrenians. The Cyrenians are a small, charitable organisation, who provide shelter for single homeless people, whom other charities turn away. In Coventry, where she helped them, they were almost all on methylated spirits, and were literally down and out. One Christmas, she stayed there for a month or so, right over the holiday, so that she could help give them a happy Christmas. She appealed for food, and to our amusement, subsequently rang Audrey saying: 'This place looks like Harrods Food Hall, people have given so much!' On a couple of occasions we went up and spent a night with them all, in the crude shelter which was all the Cyrenians could give them. The first time we were there, someone drew a knife, but Caroline, who is small and petite, just went up to the man and said gently to him, 'Come on, now, give that to me.' Later that evening, one of the men was talking to me. He was drunk, and his speech was blurred, but he pointed to Caroline and said, 'Don't you worry, Guv, we'll look after her.' These were men who, in the world's eyes, had sunk to the lowest, but in that remark there was something noble.

The smell in that shelter was awful, for most of the men were incontinent, and the mattresses were hardly ever cleaned. Audrey once asked Caroline, 'How on earth do you stick it?', to get the reply, 'Well, somehow you just get used to it.' There was the occasion when Caroline and another helper were giving them supper, and Audrey commented on the hole through the loaf of bread. Caroline explained that they couldn't keep the mice away. She then started spreading margarine on the bread with the back of a spoon, at which Audrey remonstrated. But Caroline retorted, 'Mum, with these men we don't have knives.'

Sometimes Caroline used to go to court with them. Once one of the men had been had up for some minor offence. The judge asked him why, to get the reply, 'Well Sir, you know it was like this. The doctor gave me some pills because I wasn't well, and then I had something to drink, and the trouble was that the two didn't mix, so I didn't really know what I was doing.'

'Well, what are you going to do about it?' The Judge questioned.

'Well, give up the pills, of course,' came the reply.

Caroline married and now lives in a lovely village in Worcestershire. Rowan, her oldest child, is seven, and she has two daughters of five and one. Subsequently Charlie, too, married. He works in the City of London, despite having always said that, whatever happened, he was not going to follow in my footsteps.

# 4

# Christian Marriage
# —by Audrey Arbuthnot

When I was first asked if I would write about some of the things we have learnt in marriage my heart sank! But with the family's persuasion I finally agreed.

As you have read, I met Andy in Sprimont Place before going on with him and others to Wimbledon. We always say we met on the Centre Court at Wimbledon—it sounds good! Soon after this he asked me out to dinner. Later he asked me what I thought was the strangest question, did I believe in God? I remember thinking what an extraordinary thing to ask. No other boyfriend had ever thought of asking me that, but it made me realise there was a depth and a faith in him which I respected.

He was in an emotional muddle, and when we became engaged it was quite a traumatic time, because one minute he was certain he wanted to marry me, and the next minute he panicked. We had known each other for over a year before we were married on 9th August, 1952. The night before we were married, I rang up, and Andy had gone out; for one moment I thought, 'Oh, he's panicked again.' But I was wrong and we had a lovely country wedding with two best men, one having had a motor accident on the way, and being unable to make it on time, so another friend stepped into the breach. As Andy has told you, we then went three on a honeymoon!

Prior to marriage, because of the traumas, I came out all over in a rash, and I spent the fortnight before the wedding in bed on antihistamine pills. The rash only subsided after the first week of our honeymoon and I was then bitten with the largest mosquito bites you ever saw, all over my face, and Andy went down with a high temperature. So I found myself in Spain, covered in bites and with a newly-acquired sick husband, and thinking, it's not exactly a bed of roses, this marriage business.

So many people, through upbringing and tradition, think that marriage is the be-all and end-all of everything, and that they are failures if they don't marry. I had a career, and I could only have given this up through my deep love for Andy. When we are young we can be pressurised to marry, and people are often looking and wondering if this or that person is the right one for them. If we are constantly thinking about marriage we can so easily get caught up with the wrong person. How glad I was to have had a purpose in life before meeting Andy. Looking back I see how wonderful the Lord was, bringing Andy and myself together and how there has been a thread throughout our two lives, drawing us together, which He has never let go of.

After a couple of years of marriage, our first child, Caroline, was born, and soon after, we moved from London to the country, and our second child, Charles, arrived. We made mistakes bringing up our children, as most parents do. At that time we didn't really take in that they were God's children, and that we shouldn't be possessive with them, but should think of ourselves as guardians, with our children on loan to us. This was to be new to us. Our children were a great joy always, even when they were naughty. I remembered my headmistress at school had said that children needed to be naughty as it showed character; I didn't call this to mind when they cut each other's hair or chopped up the new stair carpet!

Later we were to learn that when children are ready to leave the nest, we must let them go. If you let your child go, he or she will come back to you, but if you try and hold them they will go from you. I found it difficult to let Caroline go. We had done so much together, and all through her riding days I had given up time to trail her and her horse and horsebox round the countryside. As a family we had all walked together, holidayed together and enjoyed many activities together. It was after our last holiday together in Scotland that Caroline went away to University, and then, instead of coming home for the vacations, she went off with friends, and did various jobs. These included, amongst other things, working with the Richmond Fellowship, the Cyrenians and caring for mongol children. Although we took a great interest in all she did, having a party at home for deprived children, or going to spend a night with the down-and-outs in Coventry, part of my life had gone. Then when Charles left school, and after working in a factory, went off to France to work in a hotel, I felt lost and miserable. At this stage I started turning inwards. Caroline was the first to notice this and said: 'Mummy, why don't you find something to occupy yourself with? Why don't you get some sort of job?' I thought: 'What on earth can I do?' It was so long since I had done any work.

One day some friends came to lunch, and the wife talked about the Samaritans. She was helping in the Guildford branch, so why didn't I join? My immediate reaction was: 'They would never accept me, I don't know the first thing about counselling.' However, to Andy's surprise, I said, 'I'd like to try.' I had an inner nudge that I should do it. Later we realised what a preparation it had been for the London Healing Mission, and how the Lord had been equipping me. I did the course, read many books on psychology and counselling, and became absorbed in the work. I did both day and night duty, and found it really rewarding. About this time I was also asked to join the Board of the Royal Hospital and Home for Incurables at Putney, a Home caring for about two hundred and fifty people in wheelchairs, many of them with multiple sclerosis or suffering from road accidents. I became Chairman of the House Committee and Vice-Chairman of the Board. The Lord was continuing to equip me. Moreover through all the business travelling with Andy, going to different countries, and seeing different cultures,

He was quietly preparing me for the work He was going to lead me into.

As I realised my loss when Caroline and Charles first went away to school, I saw that I had thought being married would solve everything: provided I had Andy everything would be fine. But a husband cannot fulfil everything a wife needs; there are things one can start looking for in a partner which only God can satisfy. I think both Andy and I looked for something in each other which neither of us could fulfil, and we expected too much from each other. It is then that marriages start to break down, and ours went through a difficult patch. Caroline and Charles never realised this, because we were determined not to show it. If there are disagreements, thrash them out in the privacy of your own room! It is so important that children should feel secure, through the inevitable ups and downs of marriage.

For a long time I had thought that the emotions and make-up of a man were the same as for a woman. I could never understand why Andy couldn't see things as I saw them. But what we women so often fail to realise is that men often put their jobs before their wives. Andy did when he was in the City. A man's job may mean so much to him—after all he is the breadwinner. But a woman will very often put her husband before her home. This is a fundamental difference, and shows the importance of the wife taking an interest in her husband's work. He should equally take an interest in the home where the wife may spend much of her time. I came to realise, too, that a man puts things into compartments. He can switch from one compartment to another, and as he does so he will switch off from the first. A woman cannot do this. Her whole personality and emotions are as one.

It was one day in 1967, after fifteen years of marriage, when I had felt that everything I did was wrong, and Andy seemed so remote, that I prayed to the Lord and asked for help, as I was so unhappy. I remember quite clearly the Lord saying: 'When Andy comes home, rush out, welcome him, and show your love for him.' I had to steel myself to do this, not knowing what reaction I would get. I did as the Lord

43

said, and we all had a very relaxed and happy supper together in the dining-room. After supper Andy suggested we had a talk. We sat together and talked, and talked. Andy said he was worried about me; would I agree to put the Lord first in our marriage and try again? My answer was: 'Yes.'

We have come to realise more and more what it means to put God first and our partner second. He showers us with every blessing if we do this. As long as we yield to Him, believe in Him and trust Him, He will transform any marriage in the way He has transformed ours. But if we take our eyes off the Lord things start to fall apart again.

To give an illustration of this, a woman came to see me at the Mission. She had decided she could not cope with her husband any longer because he did not love her, and she had left him three months earlier. She had moved out from the home. As I talked to her I tried to show her how wrong this was. They had been joined together by God, and He wanted their marriage to be perfect. 'But', she said, 'my husband is not interested in me any more.'

'Perhaps not,' I said, 'But God is. If you pray to the Lord for the healing of your marriage, and go back to your husband and put loving your husband before every earthly thing, and do all you can to make your husband happy, not thinking about yourself but asking the Lord to make you the perfect wife in his eyes, I am sure you will find things will change.'

So she went back. The next time I saw her, she said, 'I know now it was right to go back. Since I have put the Lord first, and tried to put my husband before myself, he has started to react so differently, and he suddenly seems concerned to please me. I know now the Lord heals relationships.'

Sometimes, people will have married and then one of them becomes a Christian. Perhaps the wife becomes a Christian, and she is faced with the problem of how to react to her husband who still doesn't believe. Paul mentioned this situation when writing to the church in Corinth, and he wrote: 'The unbelieving husband is brought nearer to God by his believing wife.'[11] Peter also wrote of the believing wives 'Your husbands . . . may be won over without talk by the behaviour of their wives.'[12] If you do come to know the Lord yourself, it's no good nagging your husband or dragging him off to some evangelistic meeting, trying to convert him. I think one has to win one's husband for Christ by showing His love in the home. I know that for my part, I really became a Christian through seeing the change in Andy's life; it wasn't anything he said to me. We need the love and the fruit of the Spirit, and so win our partner over. 'By their fruits you shall know them.'[13]

We have learned that if you have the Lord in your marriage you can go to Him through all times of trouble and disagreement—all marriages have their times of going through the valleys as well as being on the mountain tops—and He will sort them out for you. There are always ups and downs in marriage, and the Lord grows us through these. It is no good walking off at the first sign of difficulty. You need to take it to the Lord. That's why it is essential for married couples to pray together. Things can be ironed out by both going to the Lord about them. We find that we have got to know each other in a deeper and more real way than ever before by praying together. It is as each of you opens up to the Lord, and prays aloud, that you experience a closeness to each other that cannot come in any other way.

This is an area where the husband needs to take his place as head of the wife, as Christ is head of the Church.[14] The husband must assume the spiritual headship of the family. We have people coming to us here where you can see at once that the wife wears the trousers. In this instance we tell the wife that she must not take the lead, but must gently push her husband into the position of head of the family. Great are the rewards in marriage if a husband takes his rightful place, takes the initiative, and leads them both in prayer.

St Paul writes about wives, 'Wives, submit to your husbands.'[15] Wives should back up their husbands. If you are married to a dynamic husband, for instance, and you are the quieter personality, you can do a lot to keep him on an even keel. The Lord likes a quiet and gentle spirit. If, however, you have a weak husband, don't sit on him but encourage him and build him up. Meanwhile, a husband in earlier times was one who cultivated the soil and cared for it. This is where we get our word 'husbandry'. In the best of marriages this is the sort of husbanding that is needed—cultivating all that is good in his wife and helping her to grow as a real person. In doing this *he* will be blessed.

Someone once wrote these words: 'When God made woman, He did not take her out of man's head, to lord it over him; nor out of his feet, to be trampled on by him; but out of his side, to be equal with him; from under his arm, to be protected by him; and from near his heart, to be loved by him.'

There is a unique role for us as wives which no one else can fulfil. The Lord has created us to help and encourage our husbands, and to show through our love something of the infinite love the Lord has for them. We read about this in the Creation story. The Lord made the animals, male and female, and then He made man. Then He saw that man was alone and so He made a helper suitable for him.[16] In the Authorised Version the words used are a 'help meet' for him. These words, used fifteen times in the Bible, always refer to help derived from God. Eve, the first woman, was made, that she might be a channel through whom God could work to help Adam.

Many people come to us with marriage problems. One problem is unfaithfulness. We need to be clear where infidelity starts, for infidelity starts long before one of the partners actually commits adultery with someone else. Infidelity begins when either party, husband or wife, has any form of relationship with somebody of the other sex which is not totally shared with his or her partner. Other problems in marriage are money, drink, and not being open with each other. For a marriage to succeed each partner must make him or herself vulnerable to the other. The young, or not so young, for that matter, often decide to get married being carried away by their emotions. Alternatively they may live together before they know each other properly. This often leads to a break-up. It is really important to get to know each other as friends, without a physical relationship, so you build up a mature love for each other before marriage. Emotions are so unreliable. The feeling of love can ebb and flow according to circumstances, whereas a mature love is one which moves from the emotions to a stable and basic fact. Love in marriage needs to mature beyond the feeling until it matures into fact.

Curiously, we find when we are counselling a man and wife who are having problems in their marriage, that the one aspect we don't spend much time on is the relationship between the husband and wife. We find that if we can help the husband to get his vertical relationship right with the Lord, and this usually means repentance and recommitment to Him, and if we can then go on and do the same with the wife, then the relationship between the two of them, one with the other, will slot into place. We ask them, 'Who comes first in your life?' There will often be a long pause while they think. Then we say: 'The Lord must come first and your partner second.' They must lift their eyes to the Lord and pray: 'Lord, help me to be the perfect wife/husband in your eyes.' Too many people when they go into marriage think, 'Is he or she the right husband or wife for me?', instead of praying and saying 'Lord, am I the right wife or husband for him or her?'

As we counsel people we see that forgiveness is one of the most difficult things they find. We try to tell them to put themselves in the other person's shoes, and ask the Lord to help them to forgive.

After counselling people with marriage problems, we sometimes give them the following to take away:

*A marriage must be created*

It is never being too old to hold hands.
It is remembering to say 'I love you' at least once a day.
It is never going to sleep angry.

47

It is having a mutual sense of values and common objectives.

It is standing together facing the world.

It is forming a circle of love that gathers in the whole family.

It is speaking words of appreciation and demonstrating gratitude in thoughtful ways.

It is having the capacity to forgive and forget.

It is giving each other an atmosphere in which each can grow.

It is the common search for the good and the beautiful.

It is not only marrying the right person, but being the right partner.

# 5

# From Politics to Ordination

Andy now resumes the story and he writes:

Meanwhile, back in the late fifties, something was still lacking in my City job. The work was more interesting now as I grew more experienced and then became one of the two junior directors. The firm was growing, and we were prospering. But, at the back of my mind, I had always wondered about politics. When we moved to Tilford, I had joined the village branch of the Conservative Association, and in due course I became Chairman of the Constituency Association. It must have been about 1957 or 1958 that it occurred to me that I might be able to combine earning my living in the City with being a Member of Parliament. So it came about that in March 1959 I was adopted as prospective Conservative candidate for Houghton-le-Spring in County Durham, in the middle of the coalfields. Six months later I found myself up there fighting the General Election of 1959.

The local paper was friendly; they sympathised with Harold Macmillan's government, and they wanted to see it returned. Much was the help I had from their hands. Early in the campaign they sent out a press photographer to take a photograph of me, where I was staying. I was in fact staying in a borrowed caravan parked in the farmyard of a local Conservative supporter. The photographer chose to take my photograph as I was sitting, in the sun, on the steps of the caravan peeling potatoes. That was no faked pose. I was doing my own cooking, mainly corned beef and potatoes, fried up quickly. But in order to cook the potatoes, I had to peel them. However, after they published this photograph, the editor told me with some amusement that they had had some twenty telephone calls the following morning, claiming that everybody knew that all Conservative candidates were rich and that it must have been fabricated to have had a picture of a Conservative candidate living in a caravan, and peeling his own potatoes.

About halfway through the campaign we had arranged for our two children to be looked after, so Audrey could come up and join me. We stayed at the opposite end of the scale in the home of the President of the local Conservative Association, a splendid, eighteenth century mansion. For the latter part of the campaign we lived in luxury!

At the previous General Election, the complaint had been that the Conservative candidate had never been seen, and we were determined this was not going to be said about me. We equipped ourselves with the largest rosettes we could find, a good eight inches across, and wore them firmly pinned in our buttonholes right through the campaign. None of the miners—or 'pitmen'—would come to my meetings, so I made a point of getting the Coal Board's permission to speak at the pit-head in each of the collieries in the division. I formed a great respect and indeed affection for the coalminers. Naturally, as one was walking within the coalmine to the pit-head, I passed many a miner on the way, and invariably I said 'Good Morning', or 'Good Afternoon'. Without exception, I had a courteous and cheerful greeting back from the miner I was passing. They were fair, too, over questions. I remember once when I was addressing a group of some thirty miners at the pit-head, all of them ready to go down on shift. The questioning grew heated, and several of them were throwing questions at me. I only had to say once, 'Be fair, there are many of you and only one of me; I can only cope with one question at a time.' From then onwards the questions came just as strongly, but one at a time. I liked those men.

I think the first time that I spoke at a pit-head after Audrey came up, she was waiting about a hundred yards away. As I spoke, I saw a man walk up to her and engage her in conversation. Foolishly, I hadn't warned her of the ways of the press, and I saw her expounding cheerfully as the man questioned her about how she felt as the candidate's wife. Fortunately, the reporter, for such he was, was from the local paper, but the interview that he held with her was carried in the paper the following day, under the headlines 'Mrs Arbuthnot found "rough Northerners" happy and friendly'.

In addition to speaking in the pits, we were determined that I should be seen and heard throughout the constituency. We hired a powerful loud-speaker, and wired it into the boot of the car, where we ran it off the battery. With a hand microphone and the help of this loud-speaker, I delivered a set-piece three- or four-minute speech at every street corner in the whole constituency. If they didn't see me, they were certainly going to hear me.

One day we asked the local office of the National Coal Board if we could go down one of the pits and see how the men worked. We were each given numbered metal identity disks in case of accidents and dressed up in safety helmets and overalls. We seemed to go down in the lift for a long way; then we travelled quite a distance in a truck underground, to be told we were now two miles out to sea. I was taken up to the coalface, leaving Audrey behind. They were blasting at the pit-face with a series of explosions, and I think she was quite relieved when I got back to her.

However Houghton-le-Spring was a very left-wing area. The local council had twenty-eight members, of whom twenty-seven were Socialists, and the twenty-eighth was a Communist. Quite often, while speaking at the street corner, you would see a window opening, or a door ajar, and you knew that people were listening. But they were afraid to come out into the open and be seen to be listening to the Conservative candidate for fear of what their neighbours might think. Great was our joy, therefore, one morning when I was speaking at a particular street corner, and we saw a little old lady come right out of her house at the other end of the street. Moreover, it was quite obvious that she was listening to the blaring political tones which were coming out of the

51

loud-speaker. That really cheered us up. What cheered us even more was when she started to walk towards us. She walked the whole length of the street, some hundred yards or so, she came right up to us, and greeted us. 'Ah,' I thought, 'at least here's one person who has been persuaded by my rhetoric, and who I can be confident will vote for me on polling day.' As she greeted me, I saw that she was beginning to look rather closely.

'Funny,' she said, 'I thought you were an older man: you look quite young.' I assured her that despite my youthful appearance, I wasn't really too young.

'But I thought you were quite a lot older', she went on. Then she looked at me and said, 'You *are* the Labour candidate, aren't you?' Sadly, my hopes of having one sure vote, when polling day came round, were dashed to the ground.

Part of the fun of electioneering, in a place like Houghton-le-Spring, lay in the crowds of children who gathered round to see this strange spectacle of a young man with a brilliantly-coloured rosette talking through an enormous loudspeaker. I remember one day, one of the children was bolder than the rest. Could he have a go, he asked. Little suspecting, I handed him the microphone, and foolishly I left the loud-speaker switched on. Great was our consternation, Audrey's and mine, when the words echoed down that particular street with childish clarity, 'Vote Labour!'

As you get to know people in different parts of England, you realise that even to this day, there are traces of the different races which went originally to make up our country, and one realised the different make-up of the people in County Durham. They were a splendid lot, down to earth, and they called a spade a spade. Their language when they got excited was, for a Southerner, completely impossible. I remember stopping once to ask a man the way and being directed to go round the corner and 'Gang oop-bank'. It took a little deciphering to work out that he was trying to tell us, having rounded the corner, to proceed uphill. Then there was the occasion, on polling day itself, when our little secretary, an elderly spinster who was wildly enthusiastic for all things Conservative, had been down to the local polling station. She ran back, and burst into our committee room with the news that, 'Arbooty's deeing areet!' In cold print, that may be fairly easy to decipher, but we had to have the good news explained to us, that in her view, Arbuthnot was doing all right.

In the event, the Labour candidate, who was a nice elderly ex-miner called Bill Blyton, got in with a larger majority than at the previous election. We put the Conservative vote up by 10 per cent, but one learned afterwards that by fighting the election (in the words of the local editor) 'as if we meant to win it', one stirred up opposition. Apparently, the local Labour party turned out their supporters in greater strength than in any election since the war. Consequently, although we put up the Conservative vote, we stimulated the Labour party to put their best foot forward, and their majority was in fact increased.

Although we still didn't know the Lord personally, we prayed. We didn't yet pray together, but we each said our prayers, and I remember that for several years after that general election, I prayed, and I prayed, that God would lead us to a safe constituency, where I could be adopted as Conservative candidate. Indeed, we went round to a number of selection committees, and were interviewed several times.

Then I remember going to a Conservative training weekend up in Yorkshire. I left the office in the City in a hurry, and settled back to enjoy the long train journey from King's Cross. As the train sped through the countryside, it became quite clear to me that I was chasing after something that wasn't right. It became quite clear that the deep inner desire to become a Member of Parliament simply wasn't there any longer. The desire had evaporated, and there was nothing left. I realised that for quite a time, perhaps a year or more, I had just been driving myself on, in the memory of what I had felt was a real calling. By the time I had got to Yorkshire, I had given up all thought of becoming a Member of Parliament. I talked it over with Audrey when I got back. I think

53

there were ways in which she was sad; she has always been good with people, and she felt sad that there would no longer be a chance of my holding a position of responsibility in some future Conservative administration. But she was already realising how little family life is possible for a Member of Parliament. On balance she was happy with my decision to drop it. 'Anyhow,' she said, 'if you change your mind, you can always pick it up again.' But I never did. Audrey has always been wonderful in supporting me in my decisions.

For years, I had felt cross with God for not having answered my prayer for a safe Conservative seat. It was only later that I realised that He had answered. God knows us so much better than we know ourselves. As Isaiah wrote, some two and a half thousand years ago, 'As the heavens are higher than the earth, so are my ways higher than your ways', declares the Lord.[17] I realise now that the Lord answered my request for a safe constituency, and the answer, in His mercy and His loving kindness, was 'No'. I'm more certain now, than ever before, that the Lord does answer prayer. But He only answers prayer when that prayer is in line with His will.[18] We may just as soon expect water to flow uphill, as look for an answer to a prayer which is contrary to the perfect will of God. We never get anywhere if we try to manipulate the Lord in our prayers.

Looking back on those early years of our marriage, I think we would both say that our values, then, were false. I know that for perhaps the first ten years of our marriage—I feel ashamed that it should have been so long—I was still preoccupied with the need to be accepted, the desire to be popular and to have friends. I know that at home in the country I wanted to go to the right parties, to meet the right people, and to be amusing in what I said. Looking back on those days I was worshipping at the altar of false gods. My thoughts at the time were self-centred.

I think that Audrey, too, got things out of proportion. She had a passion for cleanliness and beauty in our home. There mustn't be a spot of dust anywhere. The children always had to be turned out scrupulously neat and tidy, and I remember her standard of cooking was tremendously high. I still remember the hours which Audrey spent in the kitchen, cooking what were indeed the most lovely and I'm sure extremely nourishing meals. But, as we look back, I know both of us now regret having had our priorities wrong.

Perhaps understandably, we started to drift apart. I thought Audrey was too houseproud and ridiculously sensitive. Often when I had said something without meaning any harm, she would take it the wrong way and flare up. She, for her part, couldn't see that in flaring up, she was hurting me. I withdrew further into myself, but she then felt I was drawing away from her. Thus her self-confidence was further undermined and she became more sensitive than ever. Looking back, I'm afraid I was insensitive; I thought too much about my own problems and hurts, and too little about hers. Thus, we seemed gradually to move into a position where, within our marriage, we became more and more incompatible with each other. We were finding it ever harder to get on, yet neither of us wanted our marriage to break down.

Moreover, looking back, we were probably each looking to our partner to meet *all* our needs, whereas within everyone there are certain very deep needs which can only be fulfilled when we find God. How many marriages come unstuck for this reason. First one partner realises that he or she has fundamental needs which are not really being met in the marriage relationship. Then the doubts begin to set in: is she (or he) really the right person for me? Did I make a terrible mistake in marrying? Supposing I were to find the perfect person, now, wouldn't *all* my needs be met? As one partner begins to entertain such doubts, their attitude towards the other begins to change, and the marriage, which has not been based on God, begins to drift apart.

One day in September 1967, I realised that the position was getting quite serious. The thought worried me so much that that evening, I did something I had never done before. At five past seven I walked into our local church. I went into one of the pews and knelt down to pray for Audrey. Perhaps for the first time, I had begun to be genuinely concerned for her. I was worried as to what would happen to her if our marriage did finally break down, and perhaps for the first time in my life, I prayed unselfishly for her.

As I walked back down the aisle with my footsteps echoing in the empty church, I sensed a physical feeling that I had not had for twenty-two years. Twenty-two years before, I had been training in the army. We had often gone on long route marches of fifteen miles or so in full battle order. That meant having a large pack on one's back, a pack weighed down with kit, and I remember well the utter relief, when one got back to camp, as one eased the heavy weight off one's shoulders.

I had exactly that same feeling, again, as I walked back down the empty aisle of the church that evening in September 1967. I knew then that, without realising it, I had been carrying a heavy weight around my shoulders, and I knew that that weight had been removed. I hadn't consciously asked for forgiveness of my sins, but somehow I knew my sins had been forgiven. I can't explain it theologically; perhaps the Lord in His infinite kindness, had accepted the unselfishness of my prayer, and had thus released His loving forgiveness. All I know is that two things happened at five past seven that evening. For myself, I knew that that burden had gone and my sins were forgiven. Later, I learnt that at the same time, Audrey had realised that the clouds which had been descending on her with ever greater blackness for the preceding months, had lifted. She told me later that she knew in that moment that she had to be cheerful when I arrived home and she knew that God was in the situation. She felt this peace for the first time for months.

During the next twenty-four hours, I came to have a very clear picture of a pile of rubbish—'dross' was the unaccustomed word that came into my mind—which I had left before the altar in that empty church, and I realised that that pile of utter rubbish was formed of all the sins which the Lord had lifted off my back. Subsequently, I looked up 'dross' in the Concordance. This led me to Isaiah who saw God acting in our lives like a man who was refining precious metal.[19] In the old days, the refiner brought his crude metal up to melting point, upon which all the impurities gradually floated to the surface. These were then skimmed off the molten metal, and were known as 'dross'. What was left was the refined metal. Somehow, in His amazing love and mercy, the Lord had taken forward His purpose of refining me.

As we went to bed that evening, I remember that a verse came back to me from the days when I had read the Bible, twenty years earlier. It was a verse where Jesus promised, 'Seek ye first the kingdom of God; and all these things shall be added unto you'.[20] I think I realised that to pin one's life on a promise made in the Bible was taking a gamble on two things. It was gambling firstly on the Person who made that promise still being alive today, and it was gambling on that Person being able to honour the promise He had made, as a man, so many centuries earlier. I asked Audrey if she was ready as from now to put our God first in our marriage, and to base our marriage on that promise. Having not read the Bible for so long, I didn't know the context of that promise. I didn't realise that, in the context in which that promise was given, 'all these things' refers in the first instance to food and drink, clothing and shelter. But it seemed to me, that evening, that it could well be taken to include the healing of our marriage. Audrey agreed with me, and we knelt down simply by the side of her bed; we prayed that the Lord would help us to seek His Kingdom first, and we trusted Him to heal our marriage. From that day forward, the Lord started to work in our marriage, a process which has gone on ever since, as we regularly re-commit our marriage to Him. Over the years He has rendered our marriage more perfect than I would ever have dreamed marriage could be.

To this day, whenever anyone asks us to share with them the key to a really happy marriage, we reply that the answer is to put one's wife, or one's husband, firmly in second place. The Lord must come first. Once He is put first, He gradually pours His divine love into both husband and wife, giving them a deep and lasting love for each other.

While I was at school, I used to read the Bible, and as far as

I remember, I read it for a few years after leaving school. But I found the trouble was that it kept opening at one verse, and I was determined that that verse was not for me. Always, when I started reading the Bible again (and over the years I had made several attempts to resume regular Bible reading) it seemed to open at the verse where Jesus says: 'If any one would come after me, he must deny himself, and take up his cross daily and follow me.'[21] Each time the Bible opened at that verse, I stopped reading it. But that experience, in the church in Farnham, shook me. I knew that something real had happened to me spiritually during the few minutes that I had knelt in that pew. I could see for myself, as the days turned into weeks, and the weeks into months, that the Lord was healing our marriage, and growing our love for each other. I saw that now, at the age of forty-one, I had got to take my religion out from the drawer, where it had lain neatly folded up and put away for the last twenty years. I had to take it out and look at it seriously, and I'd got to put the Lord first.

So it came about that three months later, when we were on a skiing holiday in Austria with the children, I said to Audrey one evening, 'I believe the Lord is telling me that He wants me to go into the Church.' Audrey was splendid. She had had some experience in her family of what a vicar's life can be; she felt absolutely convinced that it was not for her, and that she couldn't cope with the round of parochial duties, with the meetings, and all that is required of a vicar's wife. But she never let on what she was thinking. She merely said to me that if I felt that the Lord was leading me into the Church, then she would naturally follow, and as far as I was concerned she was behind me. Years later she told me she had been on the point of saying she couldn't cope with being married to a clergyman, when it was as if a small voice within her said gently: 'I thought you said you were going to put Me first?'

I was determined that I wasn't going to take a major step like this until I was absolutely sure. But some two years later, I felt sure. I couldn't get rid of the conviction that somehow the Lord wanted me to go into the Church, and I applied to the then Bishop of Guildford, for him to recommend me as an ordinand, that is someone being trained for ordination. That application, however, didn't get very far. I never saw the Bishop, but I was seen by one of his assistants, who eventually gave me his opinion that I was not the material of which clergymen are made. I was turned down.

However, a few months previously, we had come across an elderly priest, who was based in one of the churches in the City. To my surprise Audrey suggested my going to see him. I hesitated as I didn't really know him. However, Audrey felt sure this was right. Consequently, as soon as I got to the office, I rang him up. Within an hour I was in his room talking to him. He was splendidly encouraging, and some of the language which he used was far from clerical. 'What the hell does that Bishop think he is doing not recommending you?', was how he put it. Whether his words were blessed in Heaven, I don't know, but I do know that they brought much comfort to my heart. Furthermore, it just happened that he was a personal friend of Mervyn Stockwood, the Bishop of Southwark, and within five minutes he was on the Bishop's private telephone, telling him that here was a man he felt he should see. Some ten days later, I found myself in the bar in the House of Lords, where the Bishop had said he would see me; I waited somewhat apprehensively for the interview.

Mervyn Stockwood is a man of considerable character, and he didn't mince words. His first words when he saw me were, 'I say, can you lend me five pounds? I've forgotten my wallet.' In the event, I think he did find his cheque book somewhere in the folds of his cassock, so the loan wasn't necessary, but it got us onto a pleasantly informal footing straightaway. He started talking to me about the difficulties of a man going into the church relatively late in life. He started expounding on the difficulties, for the man and his wife, which would be inherent in the total change of lifestyle, the change from what was now quite a well-paid job in the City, to being a parish priest.

At this point I'm afraid I interrupted him, because I felt he had missed the point. Subsequently, I learnt that he liked people who stood up to him. I told him that it wasn't my idea to go into the Church, but that the Lord was telling me to, and I was therefore hoping he would recommend me. To my relief, his tone changed. He told me to go and see his Director of Ordinands, and to apply for a spare-time training course, where I could combine theological training with my City work. From that moment onwards, he accepted me and he recommended me.

Looking back on it, I just marvel again at the way the Lord's hand was in that situation. Because I had been sponsored by the Bishop of Southwark, I was ordained to my first parish in Southwark. This was much easier than starting in our home diocese. Moreover, so much has stemmed from that first parish, that I am certain the Bishop of Guildford's assistant was in fact following the will of God when he turned me down. A few months after my interview with the Bishop of Southwark, I found myself going down to a delightful country house near Alresford, in Hampshire, for a weekend of vetting, so that the church could decide whether it approved of me. There must have been about sixteen of us who were candidates on that course, and there were five 'selectors'. The three days were fun, and I liked all the selectors. One of them was Mrs Jean Coggan, now Lady Coggan, the wife of the then Archbishop of York. She was quite pressing in some of her questions. Did I pray every day with my wife, she asked? I replied in perhaps a slightly patronising way that we had tried it several times, and as far as we were concerned, it simply didn't work. She was then firm, and with great kindness and gentleness told me that I had got to make it work, that there was no substitute for a husband and wife praying together, and that it was up to me to see that it did work. She went on to say that even when her husband was Archbishop of York, he and she regularly prayed together. Subsequently, when Audrey met him over lunch, Archbishop Coggan told her that they prayed for two hours together every morning. As a result of that interview with Jean Coggan, I prayed the following day with Audrey, and I think we have prayed together every day since then. I bless Lady Coggan for her help to me.

One or two of the other selectors were rather more intellectual, and they tried to get me to intellectualise on my reasons for going into the Church. But it hadn't been my idea that I should go into the Church. When people asked me why, in my mid-forties, in the middle of a good city career, I should decide to go into the Church, I invariably replied that I hadn't been consulted about the decision. Consequently, I parried all the intellectual questions by simply saying that the Lord had told me to go into the Church, and as far as I was concerned, that was that. The Lord, in His kindness, had shown me the right words to say, in order that His will should be fulfilled, and thus I got through my selection board. Perhaps, however, it was the end of that selection conference which afforded me the most amusement. We had a car with an automatic gearbox, and carelessly I'd left the lights on the night before. Consequently, when the time came for me to leave the following morning, the battery was flat. What I didn't know, was that with an automatic gearbox you can't start a car just by pushing it downhill in gear and then letting the clutch in. However, in blissful ignorance of this, I went back into the house, and told the various clergy who were still there, of my problem. I remember sitting at the steering wheel of the car, while my selectors of the previous few days puffed away in their cassocks and dog-collars trying to get the car to move fast enough for the engine to start. As I got out of the car, the engine having remained obstinately silent, I couldn't help commenting to them what a splendid example this was of the church in action. To their credit, I think they all saw the joke.

Thus it came about that, in September 1971, I started a three-year course of spare-time theological training, along with some fifteen other ordinands. Very soon I began to realise the predicament in which I had landed myself. The business had been growing in the City. I was now one of the Managing Directors, and I was working perhaps sixty to sixty-five hours a week. It now appeared that I was meant to do a lot of reading and, in addition, I was to write an essay each week. Added to this, our children were now in their middle teens, and I had no intention of abandoning them and working all through the weekends. Children need their father as well as their mother, and I wasn't going to let them down.

It seemed that I had let myself in for something that was quite impossible to fulfil. This was to be one of the many occasions when the Lord has spoken to me through a picture. I was praying in desperation for help and He gave me a picture of the path that I was treading; I saw clearly that the path went up to the foot of great, unscalable cliffs. I remember saying to Him, 'Lord what can I do? The cliffs are right across the path'. And the Lord seemed to say to me, 'I have put you on that path; walk on it'. 'But I can't,' I argued, 'those cliffs are blocking the way'. There was no answer from the Lord, except the repeated injunction to walk where He had told me to walk. So, in faith, in my picture, I saw myself walking forward the few remaining steps until my face was almost touching the cliff wall, and all that kept ringing in my ears was the Lord's word, 'Walk!' So I took a further step forward and pushed with my hands, and it transpired that the cliffs which I saw in my mind were made of painted cardboard and, as soon as I pushed, they fell over. Thus I was able to continue walking on the path which the Lord had put me on.

I found this picture reassuring, particularly during the early days of that course when I had no idea how I was going to be able to complete it. Somehow, however, I got through. I believe I did as much of the reading as the Lord, in His mercy, wanted me to, and as it subsequently transpired, I was able to achieve the minimum number of essays.

It was recognised that some of us on that course would go into full-time ministry, while others would continue in secular employment and fulfil their role as clergymen where they worked and in their spare time. The training was the same for all of us, and many of us didn't take a decision until near the end of the course. It seemed right to Audrey and me for me to choose the second course, and be 'non-stipendiary', that is having no pay or stipend from the church.

# 6

# The Holy Spirit Moves

There were quite a few residential weekends on that ordination course, and I used to share a room with someone who became a close friend, David Abel. I remember that, after about two years, he lent me several books, beginning with *The Cross and the Switchblade*, *The Hiding Place*, and *God's Smuggler*—and this was my first introduction to the charismatic renewal. It seemed that these were books about real people, people who had experienced a new dimension in their lives, who accepted God as being a real Person who shared their lives with them, and who told them what to do, and who worked through them. There was also this curious phenomenon of 'baptism in the Holy Spirit', which seemed pretty often to be accompanied by what, on our course, we referred to in a mildly superior manner, as 'glossolalia', but which other people referred to as the language of the Holy Spirit, or speaking in tongues.[22] Audrey and I found these books fascinating, and we realised that this new dimension of life was quite definitely something which we wanted. When the time came to choose the parish to which I was to be ordained, the thought crossed my mind as to whether I should pray to go to a parish where there would be people who had experienced this renewal. I thought it safer not to pray for it, in case God didn't answer my prayer. Nonetheless, we were longing to come across real people who could help us into this new dimension.

It was about this time—to be precise, a month before I was ordained—that I remember talking to my mother about the

Trinity. I remember saying to her that I had had some experience of God in my life, I even felt that I had perhaps had some experience of the Holy Spirit. 'But', I remember adding, 'I have an almost complete blank where the second person of the Trinity ought to be.' In no way did I know Jesus.

Mervyn Stockwood, once again, was very helpful in leading us to what was to be our first parish. He made one suggestion, and we went to the parish in question. But after a day in which the vicar showed us great kindness and hospitality, we looked at each other as we got into the car, and said 'No'. It was clear that that was not for us. The Bishop then sent us to the parish of Mortlake with East Sheen, and a few days later we called on the vicar, the Rev. Bernard Jacob, and his wife, Dorothy. We felt that this was right. Bernard felt that it was right for them too. He therefore wrote to the Bishop, and I was ordained to that parish.

I owe a lot to Bernard, now promoted to being the Venerable, the Archdeacon Bernard Jacob. I think he was slightly nonplussed at my turning up as a non-stipendiary deacon and one of his team of clergy. I don't think he had had a spare-time clergyman before. But he never interfered, he gave me every opportunity, and I always felt that, if there was any problem, I could go and talk it over with him. Dorothy, too, was kindness itself. As a newly ordained deacon, I was only expected to preach once a month, but Bernard got me into the way of taking church services, and when I produced a sermon he was always encouraging. Furthermore, when I said that I felt that the Lord was calling Audrey and me to start a prayer group, he was bold enough to let us have our heads.

How well do we remember the first meeting of that group! I had announced it in a sermon in the parish church a week before, and some sixteen people gathered in the little curate's house, in Vernon Road, which had been lent to us. We had no idea what was involved in running a prayer group. We had never been to one. So I remember that we planned a little bit of everything for them. I read to them a bit out of the

Bible, we sang a hymn, we sang a couple of modern Christian choruses, I read to them a bit of Agnes Sanford's *The Healing Light*, we had a little time of prayer and we had a little silence.

If we step out in faith, believing we are in His work, the Lord is so kind in honouring our venture. When it was over, I went round the room asking each person in turn which part of the evening had helped them most. Unanimously, they all said that the silence had been the part they most enjoyed.

This made it easy for us. We didn't know how to conduct a Bible Study, we didn't know how to pray aloud, and we didn't know how to conduct a prayer group. But, if there is one thing the complete beginner can do, without risk of failure, it is to conduct a silence! Consequently, as the group met, week by week, we had a silence, and silence reigned during the whole of the prayer meeting. Subsequently, somebody told us that it would be a good thing to read something from the Bible, so we started reading St Luke's Gospel. Then we started having a bit of discussion about it, and then very, very boldly, one or two of us ventured to say a few words aloud in prayer. Thus our 'Friday Family' began, and now, ten years later, several of them are still meeting regularly each week to pray together, and we are still in touch with them.

They were so kind. They accepted us completely, and we got great support from them. I remember Mervyn Stockwood once asking me about the problem of the non-stipendiary clergyman who probably hadn't got another similarly-placed clergyman within five or ten miles from him. From whence did he derive his moral support? I don't think the Bishop, who had a clear distinction in his mind between clergy and laity, quite saw the point when I said that all the support we needed, we drew in full measure from our 'Friday Family'.

Before we had been in the parish three months, we met Priscilla. She knew of a group in the parish which she quite often attended, and which seemed to have this new dimension we had read about in *The Cross and the Switchblade*. The idea of speaking in tongues was not strange

65

to her. So the three of us, Audrey, our son, Charlie, who was living at home at the time, and I made our way one Sunday afternoon, to what I think was some sort of community centre during the week. I remember, as we stood at the foot of the stairs, we heard someone playing a guitar upstairs, and the temptation to turn tail and flee was very strong. But we said firmly that having got this far, we were going through with it. We climbed up the rather rickety stairs, and there we found Robert Beecham playing a guitar and singing choruses. Robert and his wife Daphne had recently returned from being missionaries in the Far East. Thus began our introduction to the charismatic renewal. Robert taught us brilliantly each Sunday after lunch, and we must have kept going to that group for many months.

Meanwhile, we continued 'commuting backwards' as Audrey called it. She had two homes to run, now, and on Friday afternoons she would drive up to Mortlake with all the food, cooked for the weekend, in the back of the car.

Some time in March 1975 we heard of a clergyman at Hainault, in Essex, called Trevor Dearing, and we resolved to go to one of his services. It was a weekday evening, and Audrey and Charlie called for me at my office in the City, together with Charlie's current girlfriend. But the car which had brought them there without a murmur, then refused to start. It was Charlie's girlfriend who remarked, 'Wouldn't it be sensible to pray?' If God is the God of all creation, it must presumably follow that He understands the internal combustion engine, so we prayed. I then pressed the starter, and the car started like a bird, and indeed went without any trouble for the next three months. Looking back on it, we realised that there is an Opposition, and the Opposition didn't want us to be blessed at that service at Hainault.

We had been warned to get to that service early, and indeed I think we got there about twenty minutes before it was due to start. But we didn't get there early enough. The small church was packed, and there wasn't room for us to sit together. Eventually they found two seats for Audrey and me in the rows of chairs with which they had filled the chancel. There we were, hemmed in.

We realised pretty soon that this service was something different. Everybody sang and the church was filled with the sound of people joining in the hymns. What surprised me was the way they obviously enjoyed joining in the service. There was an atmosphere of joy in that little church. This was new to us.

What I was less keen on, though, was the way that every now and then during the hymns, people would raise their arms towards heaven. This seemed to me to be exhibitionism, and I registered disapproval. But my real trouble came during the sermon. Firstly, the vicar, Trevor Dearing, wasn't dressed properly. Having been in the Scots Guards, I thought I knew the importance of dressing properly for whatever the occasion might be. He was wearing a dog-collar, but otherwide was dressed just in slacks and a jersey. In the Church of England, as I understood it, everything had to be done according to pattern, and I wasn't at all sure that I approved of this informality. Furthermore, he didn't get up, respectably, into the pulpit to preach his sermon, but he just wandered up and down the aisle, talking as he went. As far as I was concerned that definitely wasn't on. But worse was to follow. Every now and then, during the sermon, somebody in the congregation would actually interrupt, and say 'Alleluia!' This was an Anglican church, and surely everybody knew it simply was not done to interrupt the preacher in an Anglican service.

But still worse was to come! Trevor Dearing was unquestionably a powerful speaker and he worked up to a high point in his sermon. As he reached the climax several people at the back of the church actually stood up, raised their hands to heaven, and said, 'Praise the Lord!', before resuming their seats. If I'd been able to get out of the church, I would have gone out. The trouble was, though, that the church was packed, and we were jammed in. Consequently, we had no option but to stay.

At the end of the service, Trevor Dearing invited everyone who sought the laying on of hands to go up either to him, or one of his team, for them to lay hands on them. We witnessed, for the first time, the phenomenon of people actually falling backwards under the power of the Holy Spirit. Something urged me to go forward. As I went forward, I kept saying to myself, this is out of keeping with my character, I can't think why I am going. But go forward I did. What surprised me even more than my going forward, was to find that Audrey was going forward too. I remember well, when one of Trevor's team laid hands on me. I had no inclination to fall, but I remember to this day, the gentle vibration rather like a mild electric current, which filled the whole of my body. I remember being conscious that it went from my fingertips to the tips of my toes with a lovely warm, tingling feeling all over. It gradually grew less, but I was still conscious of the tingling two hours later, when I went to bed. This had certainly never been my experience in an Anglican service before! Later, as I reflected on that service, I realised that many of my prejudices were without foundation and I must discard them. I had to recognise that people were drawn to that church because they found there something that was real.

That service was on a Tuesday evening. On the following Saturday morning, I was sitting up in bed, having my quiet time of prayer, whilst Audrey slept beside me, and some words which were not English started to come into my mind. They seemed somehow to float up from my subconscious mind, and it seemed that, as I said them, I had to get them right. If I got the accent wrong, or indeed the intonation, it seemed that something made me go back and say the words again and get them right. I remember after breakfast, Audrey asked Charlie and me to go down to the greengrocer to get some cabbage for lunch. As I went, I said to Charlie that the Lord had given me the gift of tongues. I remember Charlie breaking into a broad grin and saying, 'Bother! I hoped He'd give it to me first!' It wasn't very long, however, before Charlie received the same gift.

It was about this time, that the four of us, Audrey, Charlie, Caroline and I had been having tea together in the drawing room at home. Charlie and I had been out all day—it was one of those lovely crisp winter days with the sun shining—and we were all of us relaxed and happy together. Then, about six o'clock, Audrey reminded us that we were due to go out to supper with our neighbours, and she and Caroline went up to change. As the door shut behind them, Charlie said to me, 'I say, Dad, I think I'm meant to lay hands on you.' I laughed, and in a very unscriptural way, replied, 'OK, Charlie, I'll try anything once!'

I don't really understand what came next, except that the Holy Spirit fell on each of us pretty powerfully, and there were certain clear physical manifestations as far as I was concerned. Every twenty or thirty seconds there was a gentle shaking of my whole body. It was, however, pleasant, very relaxing, and in no way out of my control.

When the manifestations of the Holy Spirit come, they are always welcome. I learned afterwards that the Society of Friends were originally nicknamed 'Quakers' precisely because of this quaking which came upon them as they met together to pray in the Holy Spirit. Other people feel a warmth spreading through their body, sometimes a tingling, sometimes a vibration. Whatever the manifestation of the Holy Spirit may be on a particular occasion, it is invariably a blessing. But we need to beware of looking for the manifestations. Indeed, if we look for such manifestations, the Lord, I believe deliberately, will refrain from giving them to us. He wants us to grow in faith: 'We live by faith, not by sight'.[23] Looking back on that evening, I don't believe that it was the physical manifestation of the Holy Spirit's presence that mattered. What mattered was that in fact He blessed both Charlie and me.

About halfway through, I heard Audrey bustling about, at the other end of the hall; and I very earnestly did not want Audrey to come in and interrupt us. I remember the Lord putting it into my mind to put a spiritual barrier across the hall. He led me to pray, saying, 'Lord, in your Name I put a barrier across the hall; Audrey cannot pass through that barrier'. Interestingly, Audrey told us afterwards, that already at that stage she was worried about our being late for dinner. She and Caroline were changing, and she felt that it was high time that Charlie and I came up and changed too. She said she wanted to come into the drawing room to tell us to stop talking, or whatever we were doing. But she told us afterwards that for some reason she couldn't explain, she stopped short at the bottom of the stairs and felt she couldn't enter the drawing room.

Meanwhile, as Charlie and I knelt together in the drawing room that day in the winter of 1974/5, we each gave our lives to the Lord more fully than we had been able to before. Audrey told us subsequently, that she noticed the difference in us, and she couldn't make it out. We seemed to be so much more tolerant of other people. In her own words we had become 'nicer, and more thoughtful'. Did we want something from her, she wondered. She remembers thinking, 'They even say "Sorry", now, if they do anything I don't like. Men just don't do that normally! I wonder what they are going to ask me to do for them.'

But as the weeks went by, and we hadn't asked her for anything, she began to think it must be some flash in the pan, and that it couldn't last. Then, after two or three months, when the change in us had lasted and indeed developed, she said to me one evening, 'Can you explain what actually has been happening in your life and in Charlie's?'

I told her that we had given our lives to Jesus.

'What does that mean?' she asked. I explained that it meant asking Jesus to come into one's heart, and letting Him take over one's life.

'Can I ask Him into my life now?' she asked.

So it came about that, that same evening, she gave her life to Jesus, surrendered to Him and asked Him to rule in her heart.

Audrey often compares this with the car driver who deliberately vacates the driver's seat, invites Jesus to take His place at the wheel, and then himself walks round and gets into the passenger's seat. Jesus knows so much better than we do what road we should follow, and if He is the driver we are safe to go wherever He takes us.

Some people can point back to a particular day when they were baptised in the Holy Spirit. I don't know when I was. It might have been on that occasion with Charlie in the drawing room at home. It might have been when I felt that lovely tingling feeling running through me at Trevor Dearing's service. It might indeed have been on that occasion the previous summer, when I asked someone to lay hands on me to be filled with the Holy Spirit, and they prayed in tongues, and nothing *seemed* to happen. Whilst I have every respect for the person who can point to a particular date and time when they were baptised in the Spirit, we must remember that there are those, like me, who have been baptised in the Holy Spirit, but who simply don't know when they were.

I believe the same is true about conversion experiences. There are many people, particularly those with an evangelical background, who will point back to a particular day, and even time, when they gave their lives to the Lord and became Christians. For somebody who has had this experience, it is lovely to be able to look back in this manner. But we must always remember that the Holy Spirit deals differently with each one of us. Each of us is unique in the eyes of Jesus. There are many, many people who are unquestionably Christians, who don't know when they actually became Christians, and certainly I would count myself among their number.

There is, of course, controversy about 'baptism in the Holy Spirit'. Indeed, I don't think the New Testament itself is absolutely clear about it. As we read in each of the four Gospels, John the Baptist referred to baptism in the Holy Spirit,[24] and Jesus told his disciples to wait in Jerusalem, and they would be baptised in the Holy Spirit.[25] These references seem to point to baptism in the Holy Spirit being a specific one-off occurrence. Yet there is the other thread running through Luke's Gospel and the book of Acts, in which it seems that being filled with the Holy Spirit is

71

something which recurs from time to time. For example, all those of a charismatic way of mind are accustomed to looking back to Pentecost, when, unquestionably, the power of the Holy Spirit was poured out upon the hundred and twenty members of the early church who were meeting together in the upper room.[26] But only two chapters later, we read that the disciples were praying together, and the house in which they were praying shook, and they were filled with the Holy Spirit.[27] There is clearly a sense in which being filled with the Holy Spirit is something which can be expected to recur on different occasions. I like the story of the great American evangelist at the end of the last century, who was accustomed to say, 'Sure, I know I've been filled with the Holy Spirit, but then I know I leak, and I'm always glad when somebody prays for me to be refilled'. Paul's words, if one goes back to the original Greek, convey the sense of continuity; he says we should keep on being filled with the Holy Spirit.'[28]

There is a tendency with some writers to describe the event of their own conversion, or the time when they were baptised in the Holy Spirit, in graphic terms. One is left with the feeling that for them there came that moment when the heavens literally opened and they saw a blinding light, had visions of the Lord and were almost lifted up into heaven. For those who have received such experiences, I thank God. They must have been wonderful. But I don't think it is always helpful to put them into print. With other people, the facts of their conversion, and their being filled with the Holy Spirit, may be just as real, but they may not have had any of the dramatic manifestations. If these are granted to us, in His loving kindness, by the Lord, then we praise Him and give Him the glory, but it is the fact, received by faith, of our conversion, and being filled with the Holy Spirit, which matters.

# 7

# On Becoming a Christian

Leading someone to the point where they make a deliberate and conscious step of accepting Jesus, the Son of the Living God, as their Lord, was something which we were never taught in our ordination training. Every now and then one meets somebody who expresses an interest in the Christian faith, but whether through doubts, or fears, they have not felt able to commit themselves to the Person who is Jesus, our Lord. The whole essence of the Christian faith lies in an intimate personal relationship between God as revealed in Jesus, and ourselves.

There are those who will lead people to Christ by the Bible, and no doubt this way is splendid. The Bible sets out categorically who Jesus was, and who He is. Through the Bible we can learn about God, and through the pages of the Bible we can learn how we are to react to Him. The trouble is, though, that if you quote the Bible to a person who doesn't believe, you may sometimes get a respectful shrug of the shoulders, or, if they are more open, they may actually say to you, 'But if the Bible says it, so what? As far as I am concerned, the Bible is a collection of very ancient writings, and I'm unconvinced of its relevance today.'

Again, you can sometimes lead someone to Christ by telling them about the cross, that Jesus died on the cross for our sins, and that God, in the person of His Son, loved us so much that He voluntarily died there for us. There is no doubt that the heart of the Christian faith is the cross. But, to the non-believer, the fact that one more man was crucified two thousand years ago, may have been bad luck for him, but may not seem particularly relevant for themselves today.

Although we cannot prove that there is a God, the Christian faith is self-authenticating. Once one has taken the step of faith in accepting the Lord, then as one moves on in His love, and is guided by Him, the further one goes, the more one realises that the whole Christian faith hangs together logically. The further you go, the more convinced you are that it is the truth. But, this is not logic, because it is based on a hypothesis, which is the assumption that God exists. You can't prove that God exists.

I think we have a clue in the fact that man seems to be a spiritual animal. Historically, men have always groped after the infinite, following one religion or another. Historically, it has been seldom that any large number of people, for any length of time, have remained atheist or even agnostic. Furthermore, even today, when we are accustomed to the fact that we live in a materialistic civilisation, one doesn't have to look far to be aware of the spiritual stirrings that go on in people's hearts. Alongside the present renewal in all the mainline churches, there is an increasing interest in the occult, (which is in the world of the spirit, although not of God). There is a growing interest in spiritualism, and even in Freemasonry. There is certainly an increasing interest in other religions. All these things, I think, point to the fact that man is a spiritual animal, and that there is something in man which seeks satisfaction on the spiritual plane, and is restless until it finds it.

If you carry this argument further, you often reach the point when a person will realise that there is something deep within them, a deep longing if you like, to accept some sort of faith. They may be held back by doubts or fears, or there may be intellectual hang-ups, but very often a person will recognise that deep down within himself, even if he can't believe, he would actually like to believe. Certainly this is borne out in times of war. When men (or women) are in danger, whatever they think they believe, or don't believe, they pray! Indeed, in a Gallup poll, not long ago, it was

74

shown that, whilst the majority of people in this country no longer believe in God, well over 50% of them think it as well to pray to Him from time to time. There is this desire, if you like, to believe even if we feel we can't—the feeling of how nice it would be, if only we had a faith. Where has this desire come from? Why is it there?

As human beings we have all sorts of basic desires. Basic to the needs of our body is the desire for food. We call this hunger. Biologically speaking, the body needs a certain quantity of food if it is to survive and flourish. We see that this desire for food has been given to us as a means of stimulating the body to eat the food it needs.

Similarly, the human body—which is composed to quite a large extent of water—needs to take in water at regular intervals. As we all know, if we don't take in enough liquid, we are aware of the desire called 'thirst'. That desire is given us so we may take in the right amount of liquid in order for us not to suffer from dehydration. Again we all know that the human body needs a certain number of hours spent in sleep. Tiredness is, in a true sense, a desire—a desire for rest and relaxation, which is what the body needs.

You can see the same desire where procreation is concerned. If nobody got married, and nobody ever had children, the human race would die out within a few decades. Consequently, in order to keep the human race going, there is implanted in each of us a certain sexual desire, which leads to us marrying and in due course, to the arrival of children.

All these desires have been put into the human being to ensure that the human body gets what it needs to flourish and for the race to continue. Is it impossible that the desire to believe, has actually been put into the human being by the same creator God, and that it is yet another desire which it is *right* for us to satisfy?

A prominent Australian psychiatrist has written a book recounting how he went round the world, seeking wisdom from men of other cultures. He quotes a remark made to him by a wise old man in India: 'In your western civilisation, you have over-stimulated both the reasoning power of the brain and the retentive power of the brain, and as a result, you have left the intuitive power atrophied.' How terrible to think that a vital part of the human brain is often left with no more life in it than a stone.

We may therefore be able to lead someone to accept that, in the same way that it is right to follow the physical desires of hunger, thirst and so on, so it can be right to follow the intuitive desire the soul, the desire which knows instinctively that the soul will find no rest until it finds spiritual satisfaction.

It is possible, of course, that that desire for spiritual satisfaction has arisen in the soul through sheer blind fate. It is possible that there is no God, and that the human soul is just groping for it knows not what. But it is also possible that a beneficient creator God has given us that desire, because He longs both for His own sake and for ours, that we should accept Him and love Him.

The story is told, moreover, of the Christian and the Atheist, both of whom were lying on their deathbeds. The Christian is said to have turned to the Atheist and remarked, 'I have given my life in this world to the Christ I believed in, and I have received so much joy and fulfilment as a result, that, if you are right after all, Mr Atheist, and if there is no God, I will have lost nothing. But,' the Christian went on, 'If you, Mr Atheist, are wrong, then you, for your part, will have lost everything.'

The only risk we are running, if we have followed the argument this far, is that we may, in a sense, be deluding ourselves by following what we want to believe, by following what deep, deep down within our hearts we instinctively yearn for. But, as the Christian said in that story, if, at the end of our lives, we were to find that, after all, our assumption about the existence of God was wrong, we wouldn't in fact have lost anything. Indeed, we would have gained much richness in our days upon this earth.

But, if we take that step of faith and say, 'I am prepared to accept that there is a God; I am prepared to commit myself to You; and to ask You to reveal yourself to me,' then, as I said

76

earlier, the Christian faith becomes self-authenticating. The further one goes, in accepting Christianity, the more it all hangs together, the more one reaches the point at which one no longer says, 'I believe', but instead one changes to saying 'I know'. Years ago, I remember seeing a programme on television, when a young man in his early twenties was being interviewed. I remember the last question, just as the programme was ending: 'So you really believe then, that there is a God who loves you?' As the picture faded, I have always remembered his reply, 'I don't believe. I know.'

God's infinite love extends to men of every faith and of none, and all the world's great religions are reflections of men seeking after God. But is it true that Christianity is the highest revelation of God's nature and the most true? There are difficulties with the Moslem faith. Essentially Mohammed portrayed a remote god of anger rather than a God of such infinite love that he desires us to call Him, Father. He denied the fact of Jesus' death on the cross. Moreover, Mohammed laid down that each man might have a total of four wives. The highest ideal must surely be monogamy, a single man and wife joined together by God for life; the idea of a man being able to take up to three more subsidiary wives seems degrading. Furthermore, a faith that, when originally propounded, encouraged its men to go fearlessly into battle against the infidel, assuring them that if they died in battle, they would go straight to paradise, where they would have an unending supply of young ladies to enjoy themselves with, doesn't really seem to compare with Christianity.

There is then the Jewish faith, out of which, of course, Christianity grew. The Jews indeed share a number of books in our Old Testament with us. But for the Jew, so often God is still a remote being, awesome, indeed, in His holiness, but remote. The idea of God being a heavenly Father, who loves us deeply, is still often foreign to the practising Jew, whilst the intricate laws, which a strict Jew has to follow, and which govern most aspects of his life, somehow don't seem to meet the needs of our everyday life.

Then, as one moves further East, one comes to the two great religions of Buddhism and Hinduism. Both of these tend to ignore pain. There is much suffering and poverty in India because of the fatalism that both these creeds embrace. In no way do either of these great religions preach the gospel of loving one's neighbour as one loves oneself. Whilst the centre of the Christian faith is undoubtedly a living personal relationship with God as revealed in Jesus, yet, as James in particular tells us in his letter, our faith needs to find practical expression in love for our neighbours, and in compassion for those who are less well off.[29] This compassion is not fundamental to either the Hindu or Buddhist religions.

The gods of the Hindu religion are almost without number. There are gods, goddesses and godlings, numbering a thousand and more. Of the major gods, one is an elephant and one is a monkey. This seems to me a far cry from the pure, monotheism of the Christian faith. Meanwhile, in Buddhism, the disciple is taught to subjugate all desires, so that by killing desire, he may reach a stage of having no desire at all; he seeks to find peace, in what in some ways, can only be a sort of suspended animation, as he sits there, cross-legged, contemplating his navel and waiting for his disciples to bring him such food as is necessary to keep his body going.

Travel farther East, and you come to the religions of China and Japan. But these are more in the nature of philosophies. In no way is there a parallel in these faiths, nor is there indeed a parallel in any other world religion, of what we find in Christianity, namely that God is a God of love, a loving Heavenly Father, who, Himself, has sought us out because He longs to have a relationship of love with each of His children. Moreover only Christianity tackles the basic problem of man's own dissatisfaction with himself; only Christianity tackles, head-on, the problem of sin.

Each of the world's major religions is indeed an expression of mankind seeking after God, but only Christianity is an expression of God in His love, seeking after men. Only Christianity reveals that it is in the very nature of God for Him to love. All of us need to be loved and to love. If we have been starved of love we may have learned to suppress this need, but we cannot quench it. The love of our family and friends can be most wonderful. But this love can never replace our need for the divine love which is revealed to us in Jesus.

But people have further difficulties about accepting the Christian faith:

1. Quite often, we come across people who are prepared to accept that there is some beneficient and impersonal power of goodness overseeing the world. Their difficulty comes, when one asks them to accept that that power is actually a Person—and indeed so much more than Person. But if that power really did create the world, then if it is not a Person, the human being, which it created, is more wonderful than it is itself. As the philosophers tell us, it is impossible for the creature to be greater than the creator. How can anybody create something which is more wonderful than they are themselves?

   Moreover, a 'thing' cannot love, and it cannot receive love. I may stand in front of a picture in somebody's house, and say 'But I just love that picture'; I can get lost in admiration for a beautiful painting. But when I say I love that picture, I don't mean that I love it in the sense that I love my wife, or my children. In the same way, that picture is totally incapable of loving me. If it is true that the highest that we, as human beings, can experience is the ability to love and be loved, then it follows logically, that God must love and must be capable of being loved, and for that to be true, it must follow that God is personal. Only a person can really love.

   If we are to satisfy that deep, inner need within ourselves, we need to find the God whom we can worship. We can only worship from the bottom of our hearts a Person who is perfect love, perfect holiness, indeed who is perfect in every way. We need someone to whom we can give ourselves in perfect love, for now, and for all eternity.

2. When people can feel the Lord's presence it is easy for

them to believe in Him. The problem comes when they can't—and for many of us, this is the situation for most of the time. I often say to people then: 'Do you believe in *me*? Do you believe that, here in this room with you, is a real live man?' Often they look puzzled as they say: 'Why yes!'

The reason they know there is a man in the room with them is because they can see me, they can hear me, and indeed if they move slightly, they can feel me. Their senses tell them I am there.

'But', I continue, 'this evening, when you're back in your home, you won't be able to see, hear or touch me. Do you think that I shall therefore have ceased to exist?'

Thus a person can come to see that the Lord exists irrespective of their senses. It doesn't matter if they can't feel His presence, He is still there, nonetheless.

3. The culmination of His love for us was when Jesus died for us and rose again. But often people have difficulty in believing that Jesus actually overcame death. What is evident from the Bible narrative is that the early disciples were convinced that He had risen from the dead. They were so convinced of the truth of this, that they made every sacrifice and faced every conceivable hardship in order to proclaim the fact of Jesus crucified, buried, and risen from the dead. They knew that their leader had been executed most cruelly, and they must have known that, if they went on proclaiming Him, the same fate would probably overtake them—as, in fact, in many cases, it did. But they didn't care. They knew the truth and they had to proclaim it.

Moreover, they were quite prepared to call their witnesses. Paul, in writing to the Corinthians,[30] lists those to whom Jesus had appeared after His death, including, on one occasion, over five hundred of the brethren at once, 'Many of them are still alive now,' he seemed to be saying: 'Come and ask them yourselves'.

A leading lawyer, Sir Edward Clarke KC has written: 'As a lawyer I have made a prolonged study of the evidence for the events of the first Easter Day. To me the evidence is conclusive, and over and over again in the High Court I have secured the verdict on evidence not nearly so compelling. . . . As a lawyer I accept (the gospel evidence) unreservedly as the testimony of truthful men to facts they were able to substantiate.'

4. Then there are those who will claim that, however much, deep within themselves, they would love to have a faith, they find it impossible to reconcile the existence of a God of perfect love with all the immense volume of suffering and pain, which there unquestionably is in the world. I find that for myself, I can only reconcile these two facts, when I remember something of the immensity of the suffering of God, Himself. We are apt to say that if a person loves someone very much, and sees that person suffering, then his heart 'bleeds' for that other person. If God is perfect love, then His heart must indeed bleed for each and every one of His children, as He feels for them in their suffering. The total of His suffering must be beyond anything we can begin to understand. That way, I can begin to reconcile a God of perfect love with all the suffering that goes on in the world.

There was a man between the wars, who said, 'God simply cannot be a God of love, because if He was, His heart would break.' He realised that if God is love, His heart must be breaking all the time, as He feels for each of us in our sufferings. The short answer to that man, is that God's heart did indeed break and that it broke on the cross. From the evidence in John 19:34-35, it is believed that the actual cause of Jesus' death was cardiac rupture. But even so, why doesn't God stop all the suffering? I think, here, one has to come back to the fact that God is perfect love, and that He longs for each and every one of His children to enter into a perfect relationship of love with Him. But even we, as human beings, know that you cannot force another person to love you. If you want somebody to love you, they have to be free to reject you, also. That is basically what has happened in the world. As

81

the great majority of the world have rejected God, the great majority of suffering which goes on in the world has come, ultimately, through man's disobedience. It seems so sad that we blame God for the pain which, in fact, man has caused and which God, Himself, suffers with us.

Furthermore, wherever you find suffering in the world, you do, in fact, find that Christians have been drawn there, to help. In the Middle Ages, all schools were originally built by the Christian Churches, and most of our hospitals were originally Christian foundations; the evil of slavery was ended after years of campaigning by a prominent Christian, William Wilberforce, and the foundations of modern nursing were laid by a Christian lady, Florence Nightingale. We read in the Gospels that Jesus showed great concern for those who were suffering; and that concern is found throughout the centuries, in those who follow Him.

Let us accept that God is perfect—perfect love, perfect holiness, perfect righteousness, perfect in every way. In classical times, the Greeks and the Romans had their gods and goddesses; those gods were like men and women in their weaknesses and in their failures, and so it was impossible for men really to worship them. If that deep, inner need within myself is going to be satisfied, I need to be certain that God is perfect in every way, that He can never let me down, that He loves me with a love that is beyond any human understanding.

If that is a fair picture of God, and if God existed before the world began, and if God indeed created the world and all the universe, it must surely follow that originally the world which He created was perfect. I cannot conceive of any person who is perfect, deliberately creating something which was imperfect. It simply doesn't make sense. Indeed, the very first chapter in the Bible bears this out, for we read that when God had created the world, He 'saw all that He had made and it was very good'.[31] Of course it was very good, because a God who is perfect had made it.

Then somehow, evil, sin, sickness and pain got in, and

spoilt the creation which God had made. You can take the story of Adam and Eve being tempted in the garden of Eden,[32] either literally or symbolically. Either way I know of no better explanation for what must originally have been a perfect creation, being subsequently spoilt by the intrusion of sin and pain, sickness and suffering. The whole essence of the story is that man effectively said, 'I know what God has told me I can do, and I know what God has told me I am not to do, and I'm simply not going to pay any attention to God. Henceforth, I'm doing what I want.' And a capital 'I' was enthroned in the place of God. That, in many ways, has been at the centre of the human problem from that day onwards. Man rejected God. As he accepted sin, he put himself under the bondage of Satan. That bondage was broken when Jesus' blood was shed for us on the cross.

God is longing, once again, to perfect His own creation in us. But as someone once said: 'He is too much of a gentleman to force Himself on us.' Many of us know Holman Hunt's picture of Jesus: 'The light of the World'. Jesus is standing at the door of our hearts, knocking. But there is no doorhandle on the outside of that door. The door handle is only on the inside. Only we can open that door and invite Him in.[33]

There simply is no doubt of the peace, and indeed the joy, which Jesus gives through His Holy Spirit, to those who truly accept Him and give themselves to Him. Part of the immense satisfaction of the work which Audrey and I do, now, is seeing people come in with faces which are drawn and empty, to go out later with that very joy.

# 8

# On 'Seeing' Jesus

We have seen that one of the greatest difficulties about the Christian faith is this: that though a personal relationship with the Lord is central, how does one relate personally to someone one can neither see, nor touch, nor (normally) hear?

Each of us is composed of body, soul and spirit. If one imagines dissecting a person, one will find their heart, liver, bones, etc., but one will never find the spirit. The spirit is the intangible, immaterial part which lives on and is indeed the real person. In our daily lives we are meeting spirits every day as every person we meet has a spirit. But we are accustomed to meeting spirits who live within a body, and the spirit of the person we may be talking to, expresses itself through the physical features of his or her body. As we see the mouth moving, as we watch the hands, as we see the light in somebody's eye and as we hear the tone of their voice, we get to know them as a person. In brief, their physical body interprets their spirit to us.

The difficulty with the Lord is that He has no physical body. How, therefore, do we enter into this personal relationship with Him, without which Christianity is but a set of arid rules? It is at this point that the imagination comes into play. We have a lot of documentary evidence in the Bible about Jesus, and it is quite possible to paint a picture, in words, of Jesus standing there before us. As one imagines His physical features, and indeed His feelings, imperceptibly one is led into the real presence of Jesus.

I usually picture Jesus as a young man, and perhaps the

first thing that strikes me is the peace which flows from Him. He was completely integrated, and at one with Himself—a young man who took himself for granted and was therefore able, all the time, to go out to those He met and whom He loved. As He stands in front of us, we become aware of His peace, and indeed of the stillness of His hands.

As we continue to look at Him, our eyes move upwards to His face. He has a dark skin, (He lived at the other end of the Mediterranean), His hair is dark brown, almost black, and would probably have been allowed to fall long over His shoulders. As we look at His face, we see no trace of weakness.

Sometimes one thinks of the phrase in that childhood hymn, 'Gentle Jesus, meek and mild'. Gentle, He certainly was. There was the occasion when the disciples (who were very much 'grown-ups') tried to shoo the children away. The children would not have crowded around Jesus unless He had been gentle. Often I think that perhaps the happiest moments in His life were when, at the end of a long day, He must have sat down in the evening light to relax, and children climbed on His knee, and He told them stories.

'Gentle' He was, but was He 'meek'? He was meek in the sense of the Greek word, which is misleadingly translated. It was a word they used for a very large and powerful warhorse, kept completely in control. As one looks at Him, one realises His tremendous power, coupled with complete self-control.

'Mild' he never was. He was devastating when He met with hypocrisy or cant, although full of love and compassion for anyone who had been harshly treated. One remembers the story of the girl who was taken in adultery.[34] Jesus was teaching in the temple at the time, surrounded by a crowd of listeners. There was a commotion and some of the temple authorities heartlessly pushed in front of them a girl who was scarlet with embarrassment and in floods of tears. One can hear their strident voices down the centuries as they cry out, 'Teacher, Moses commanded us to stone such women. What do you say?'

Jesus was always in control of any situation and His

reaction was one they had not expected. He bent down and wrote in the dust with His finger—perhaps deliberately doodling as He wanted to avoid a confrontation.

The men's courage clearly began to ebb; then, at the psychological moment, Jesus looked up and said, 'If any one of you is without sin, let him be the first to throw a stone at her'; then He deliberately went back to writing in the dust. Those men knew quite well that none of them was without sin. What was more, the crowd knew it, and they knew the crowd knew it. They slunk away one by one.

Then we come to the most amazing part of the story. The girl remained. It would have been so easy for her to have slipped away as her accusers did. By now she must have been so totally taken up with wonder at Jesus that she forgot the crowd behind her. Then Jesus looked up and said, 'Where are they? Has no-one condemned you?' 'No-one, Sir,' she replied. Then Jesus told her to sin no more—there was never any compromise with sin—but He told her to go, and to go free.

One can see in this story His compassion, and His sympathy for the girl, and one feels that His joy at seeing her go free, forgiven, came near to equalling the relief and the joy of the girl.

As we return to looking at His face, it is His eyes which really attract our attention. We see the compassion, the sympathy, the love, the power and, indeed, the longing—the longing that we, like the girl, should be washed clean, forgiven and set free.

As we meet His gaze, and as we realise that He looks through our eyes into our very souls, we become aware of His absolute holiness and of His love, and we realise that however much we fall short, (and we all do), of His standards of holiness and perfection, yet we can trust Him. In the love and the strength of those eyes, there is that which gives us complete confidence in Him.

Then, in a sense, the imagination falls away and we find ourselves opening up our hearts to Him in love and worship. As we contemplate His perfect holiness we cannot help acknowledging that we are very sinful and second-rate compared to His holiness, and so we ask for His forgiveness. Then, because we read that if we confess our sins, 'He is faithful and just and will forgive us our sins, and purify us from all unrighteousness',[35] we can acknowledge His forgiveness and the freedom which that confers. As we relate further to Him in love and in worship, we find ourselves giving ourselves completely to Him, asking Him to take over our hearts and take over our lives. By now the imagination has completely fallen away and we are relating directly to the Son of God, being aware in ourselves of the warmth of His love and freely offering ourselves to Him in love.

Many people find it difficult to relate to Jesus when they pray, and one can adapt the above method. Try reading an extract from one of the gospels, describing a scene in which Jesus partook, and read it to yourself two or three times. Then deliberately shut your Bible, imagine there is in the room with you a friend who has never heard of Jesus, and recount the story in your own words. Go further, and fill in the details, the colour of the sky, the sandy track on which they were walking, the grey-green colour of the olive trees in the background, the presence of the disciples and the crowd. Go further and describe aloud to your imaginary friend what Jesus is feeling throughout the episode, describe the expression on His face, describe the tone of His voice, and as we remember His perfect love, so it will be possible to build up this image of Jesus in one's mind. It is then but a short step to seeing oneself joining with the disciples or the crowd who were present on that occasion, and if, for instance, it was a miracle of healing, one can join with the person who has been healed and share their joy with them and share their gratitude to Jesus. So again one moves imperceptibly from the imagination into what is real and one can relate to Jesus.

Thus we realise that in a very true sense Jesus is a separate person 'out there'. Whilst theologians will doubtlessly call this over-simplification, it is often easier to think of the Holy Spirit as being that person of the Godhead who dwells within us and Jesus as being 'over there' or outside us. After all, one can only enter into a relationship of love with another person if they are separate from us!

# 9

# Chairman of a Merchant Banking Group—and After

Meanwhile the little family firm, which I had joined in 1948, had grown to quite a large financial business, employing a thousand people and with gross assets in our balance sheet of some £200,000,000. I loved running the group, and I formed friendships then which remain dear to me. We covered a wide range of services including banking, insurance broking, unit trusts, factoring, export finance, computer consultancy and personal budgeting. To cover this wide range of services, we had to have a number of different management teams, each expert in its own field. I always enjoyed trying to gain the confidence of those who headed up the different teams, and seeking to help them give of their best. There were failures, of course, and there were those who didn't come up to the necessary standard. There were always one or two who found it impossible to trust another person, and there was the appalling tragedy when one of my close colleagues committed suicide. But by and large, my recollection is of a happy group. We worked hard. We worked long hours, and we were loyal to one another. I couldn't help taking pride in seeing how the little family firm had grown into something large and prosperous, and which, while giving a fair return to our shareholders, and providing a good livelihood for a thousand people, maintained the highest standards of integrity.

I made an absolute point of wearing a tiny metal cross in my buttonhole every day in the City to make quite clear what

I stood for and people sometimes used to ask me how it was possible to combine being a clergyman and a businessman. But I didn't find difficulty in combining the two. Certainly, in the City of London, as indeed in any other large gathering of human beings, there are people who are sharks. There are people who want, as the Americans say, 'to make a quick buck', and who will cut corners. There are people who will follow standards which are less than the highest. But on the whole, I found standards of integrity in the City were high. In a way, this is a matter of self-interest. The City is a small place, and it is very easy to lose one's reputation for integrity and straight dealing. Once lost, it may take many years to recover. It is therefore in the interest of any firm to have the highest standard of conduct, so that others in the City, with whom they are doing business, may know that they can deal in confidence and safety.

The same is true of staff. An employer must always be absolutely fair to the people he employs. It is not right to overpay them, as that is squandering the shareholders' money, but equally, there is nothing clever about under-paying them. Gauging the right rate, particularly for senior jobs, can be very difficult. But I was always clear that my objective was to pay a fair rate, a rate which was fair both to the man, and to the shareholders.

I remember the Chief General Manager of one of the largest insurance groups in this country, a group with a household name, saying to me, 'It doesn't matter what the Chief General Manager of this Group does, what matters is what he *is*'.

How true that is. I was fortunate enough to have worked for many years under my predecessor as Chairman, John Prideaux, now Sir John Prideaux. He was a born leader, and had great wisdom. But above all, he had complete integrity. There were times when one was disappointed at decisions he made. There were times when one thought those decisions were wrong. But invariably, one knew whatever decision he made, he made it with integrity, believing that it was the right decision under the circumstances. Although in some ways I found him a difficult man to follow, yet he had set a splendid example, and I resolved early on, that I would try to pursue the same high standard of honesty, fairness and integrity. Not for a moment am I trying to say that I always came up to these standards, but we always need to aim for the highest. Michelangelo, that brilliant artist and sculptor of the Italian renaissance, used to pray, 'Lord, grant that I may always desire more than I can accomplish'. It is a saying which we have on the wall here at the London Healing Mission.

The hardest decisions that I ever had to take were when, as happened occasionally, a man simply was not capable of coming up to the standard which was expected of someone in his position. I recall one man in particular to whom this applied. Was it right to tell him to leave? One could argue that, ideally, it would have been right to have kept him in his job, and right for those who were working with him to have rallied round and helped him to get the best out of himself until he came up to the required standard.

But then I had to consider my responsibility towards those who were working under him. Was it fair for me to impose on them a man who was manifestly not performing as he should? Staff always know if a director, who is over them in their particular company, is incompetent. Nothing can be more destructive of morale than for them to have to work for someone whom they do not respect. I had a responsibility to them, too.

The particular person I am thinking of was a director of one of the fifty or so companies in our group. It was a company we had taken over some years before, and he was a director when we took it over. It wasn't our fault that he had been promoted above his capability. But then nor was it his. I agonised over the question of what to do with him for a couple of years, and I prayed. Eventually, I had to face the fact that continuing to keep a man in a position where he was manifestly not pulling his weight, and in which he was incapable of doing what was expected of him, was dragging down the morale of the whole team—and I had to ask him to go. Naturally, the financial arrangements which we made with him were as generous as we could justify.

It was a difficult decision. A few days later, I had a telephone call from his wife, who was quite frankly abusive. How could one expect her not to be? She believed in her husband, and she felt that he had been unfairly treated. I had every sympathy with what she was saying, but I wasn't going back on what I had decided. I continued to feel concern for him. I arranged for him to have a course of counselling, to help him adjust to the new situation, and some months later, I learned that he had got a job, but at a lower level, a level where he ought to be able to cope with the standard that was required of him. Afterwards he told one of his former colleagues that my telling him to leave had actually been a blessing.

If you are heading up a group of companies, you have of course your obligations to the shareholders as well as your obligations to the staff who work for you. The money in the company belongs to the shareholders. They have invested in your company, in the expectation of increasing dividends, and one's purpose is to provide increasing profits. Put at its most basic, that is why one is employed to run such a group of companies. During the seven years I was running the Arbuthnot Latham group, we more than doubled our annual profits, but all the while we were aware that we were too small to compete in the world of international banking. The present time is the age of enormous conglomerate banks, and we were small. Eventually, we took the deliberate decision that we would seek to be taken over by another bank which had the capital that we lacked. We completed the negotiations to this end in October 1981, and were the third member of the Accepting Houses Committee to be taken over. It was a source of satisfaction when the *Financial Times* pointed out that the two previous Accepting Houses had been sold at less than the value of their net assets, whereas we had obtained for our shareholders a price which was more than half as much again. What mattered even more to me was that the continued employment of our staff was safeguarded.

I felt that, in bowing out on that note, we hadn't done too badly.

It was only in November 1981 that Audrey and I were able to get away for a much-delayed summer holiday. We did what we've often done, just took the car across the Channel and pointed it south, without any clear plans. We find that one can always stay in one of the local French inns. They are clean, the food is always adequate and usually good, and the people are friendly. Besides, one is entirely one's own master. Eventually, we finished up in a lovely medieval village in the Alpes Maritimes, some fifty miles behind Cannes on the French Riviera. We had a lovely ten days there, enjoying the autumn sun and the clear blue skies, and both of us painting some of the views in the old village. But, as I prayed, I became increasingly aware of the words coming through in prayer, 'End of chapter'. I knew quite well what this meant. At last, after so many years, the Lord was saying to me that He wanted me to come out of the City, and to go into full-time Christian work. By now, I was ready for the move and with complete peace in my heart, I decided to leave the City after nearly thirty-five years.

It was in December 1981 that we went, with Charlie, to an evening service at Holy Trinity, Brompton. The church, as usual, was packed with some seven hundred or so people, most of them in their twenties or early thirties. The atmosphere of enthusiasm and worship was lovely, and, as always in that church, we felt gloriously uplifted as we joined in the singing and opened our hearts to praise and worship our Heavenly Father. When the service finished, the broad aisle was thronged with people meeting their friends and chatting. I remember the vicar, John Collins, whom we had met once or twice before, coming down the aisle, and I went over to have a word with him. I told him that I was thinking about coming out of the City, and that we felt the Lord was calling me to some form of full-time Christian work. He remembered the conversation, and in due course, he asked me to join him in the new post of administrator in that large and growing church. So it was that I moved straight there from the City. I finished work in the City one Friday evening, Audrey and I took off the following morning for a last business trip to Munich, where one of our most important clients was situated, and then I reported for duty at Holy Trinity, Brompton, a little late, on the Monday morning, having flown back with Audrey that morning.

John Collins, for his part, and Audrey and I, for ours, all felt clearly that it was in the Lord's will that I should take up that job at Holy Trinity, and indeed we have never had cause to doubt it. John kindly asked me to take the Wednesday Healing Services during the time I was there. However, as the year 1982 drew to a close, we became clear that it was the Lord's will that we should leave as of December 31st. As the months went by, John and I had come to see the job differently. It seemed I was not the person to do what he wanted done, whereas the job he wanted me to do was not what I was looking for. We agreed, therefore, that I should leave at the end of the year.

Audrey and I benefited greatly from our eight months at Holy Trinity, and we continue to advise people who are looking for a live, supportive church to go there, if they live anywhere in that neighbourhood. It was not an easy period, changing more or less overnight from running a large financial group to employing three girls in the Vestry, to having no secretary, and indeed having to stick the stamps on my own letters. Audrey also found the adjustment difficult. However, it was good for both of us.

Furthermore, at Holy Trinity, we were having more time for personal ministry. In a congregation which altogether numbered some fourteen hundred people, it was quite impossible for the four full-time clergy to do all the pastoring themselves; and there was a steady trickle of people who came to see me for counselling and prayer in the subterranean office I occupied below the vestry—my 'dungeon', as we referred to it. Every now and then someone would walk in to the vestry and ask if there was a clergyman whom they could see. I always suspected that the girls replied, 'Oh, yes, we have a tame one here. We keep him locked up, downstairs.' The vestry was a happy place to work in, and that further training in individual ministry was invaluable. Whenever we could, Audrey and I counselled together.

Meanwhile the Lord was preparing both of us for the next step in our lives. But preparing us for that step had started five years earlier, when we had read a book by Rev. Roy Jeremiah, who at the time had been Missioner at the London Healing Mission, and we were interested in what he had been doing. Soon after reading the book, Audrey and I were doing a Christian Leadership Course in St John's Wood. It was run by the Post Green Christian Fellowship, and roughly fifty of us would come there every Saturday, and after the first two sessions, we would break off, and each eat our sandwich lunch, scattered round the large hall in which we met. On the particular Saturday I am thinking of, I was sitting alone. I think Audrey was surrounded by a circle of friends, and I was quietly munching away, reflecting on the events of the morning, when a lady whom I had never spoken to, came up to me and apologised for intruding. She went on to say, 'I believe God has told me to tell you that you are to head up The London Healing Mission.' She then looked at the informal T-shirt which I was wearing, 'You aren't by any chance an Anglican clergyman, are you?' she asked, 'Because it does have to be one.' I laughed, and assured her that although I might not look like it, I was in fact an ordained priest in the Church of England.

We had given this quite a lot of thought at the time, but at that stage it simply did not seem right to give up the City, and to take any further the idea of working at the London Healing Mission. But now at the end of 1982, with the date fixed for my leaving Holy Trinity, the question was before us again: where was the Lord going to lead us now?

It was about then that the Rev. Tom Jewett who was the Missioner at The London Healing Mission, came to give a talk at Holy Trinity, Brompton. It just so happened that I was free that morning, and I decided to go to the talk. It just so happened, too, that when I walked into the room, Tom Jewett was standing by himself, and it just so happened that for the next quarter of an hour, he and I talked together. God works so often through seeming coincidences, that in our family we have come to refer to them as 'Godincidences'. Tom told me that he felt the Lord was calling him back to Australia, and as he told me the date for his leaving the Healing Mission, I realised it was exactly the date when I was to leave Holy Trinity.

This made me sit up, and I went back and discussed with Audrey whether it could ever be within the Lord's will that we should take over at the London Healing Mission. I discussed the question with John Collins, who was quite firm in what he said: 'I believe that the ministry to which God is calling you is a ministry of healing and deliverance.' In brief, he gave the idea his warm blessing. We also went one evening to have supper with the Rev. Nicholas Rivett-Carnac and his wife, Marigold, of St Mark's Kennington, two people whose opinion we valued. 'Yes', they said, 'we respond to what you are saying, and we believe it would be right for you to apply to succeed Tom Jewitt.' Naturally, we prayed a lot about it, and as I prayed, it just seemed to me that the words came through in prayer, 'I have reserved the London Healing Mission for you.'

Thus it came about that I found myself writing to the Trustees of the Healing Mission, telling them of those words I felt I'd heard in prayer, but acknowledging that I might very easily have misheard what the Lord was saying. I can remember finishing the letter saying that whatever decision they took, it would be nice if they would allow me to pray with them that the Lord would lead the right Missioner to the London Healing Mission. Subsequently one of the Trustees came round to see Audrey and me.

It was about three weeks later that I found myself attending a meeting of the Trustees, and I would happily have sunk through the floor, when I found myself ushered into the room to hear the senior trustee say, in no uncertain tones, 'This is the man whom God has chosen to head up the London Healing Mission'. They had, moreover, planned that there should be an interregnum of three months after

Tom Jewett left, when they would look after the Healing Mission themselves. Similarly, we had felt that having had no break after leaving the City, it would be nice for us to have three months clear at home. Thus Audrey and I moved into the London Healing Mission at 20 Dawson Place, just north of Notting Hill Gate, during the first week of April, 1983.

Within a few days of coming to the Mission, as I was praying one morning, the Lord gave me a lovely picture which seemed to confirm everything. It was as if I was several hundred feet above Dawson Place. I can remember the picture clearly. I was above No 20, and rather behind it, and I could look down on all the roofs. As I looked, I saw suspended over No 20 an enormous crown of gold. It was so big that it extended over the roof of the whole house, and was suspended probably some thirty or forty feet above the roof. It seemed that this picture was a lovely confirmation that the Lord wanted us to be here, and that He was going to bless, not our work, but His work at the London Healing Mission.

Thus we were clear beyond doubt that we were in the Lord's will in coming to the job where we are now. Looking back on it, we had first received His word from that lady, some five years earlier, we had tested that word at the time, and we subsequently came to see that it fitted in with what followed. We had then sought advice from other Christians whom we respected. The course it seemed right to take was consistent with scripture. We had sought God in prayer. Finally we had come to experience the peace and the quiet joy which the Lord gives each of us when we are right with Him. How important it is to check and cross-check in all the different ways that are open to us, that the course we are considering really is in line with His will.

# 10

# *The London Healing Mission*

People sometimes ask us what the London Healing Mission actually consists of. It's a small independent charity which was started soon after the war, but based on work which had begun in the 1930s. It is housed in a building some five minutes walk from Notting Hill Gate tube station, in London, and Audrey and I have a bedroom at the top of the house. The purpose of the Mission has always been for the Missioner to hold healing services on Thursday mornings and evenings, and otherwise to spend his days ministering to people who come here. In addition it is important for the Missioner to go out and preach when he is asked to do so, in order to help others, in other churches and fellowships, to grow into the healing ministry.

When Audrey and I came here, we saw it as a joint ministry. Indeed it is quite clear that Audrey is not here just because she happens to be my wife, but she is here in her own right, because of the healing ministry, which the Lord, Himself, has given to her. We divide the day into one-and-a-half hour periods, and we minister to people, each taking two in the morning, two in the afternoon, and one in the evening. It means a long day if one includes correspondence and the inevitable administrative jobs, and we are at it pretty well non-stop, from when we get up in the morning till bed-time at night.

Much of the power behind the London Healing Mission derives from the fact that over six hundred Intercessors all over the country pray for our work each day. Moreover, we start each day at the Mission with a time of prayer and worship, together with those members of the team who are in that day. This gives us the opportunity to pray for those who have asked for prayer or are in particular need, and we finish with Holy Communion.

Every day, perhaps a dozen or twenty people may write to us, or telephone, asking for prayer. Besides praying for them each day at the Mission, we circularise all the requests for healing once a month to the Intercessors, in such a way that each Intercessor is given the Christian names of five people who are seeking prayer for healing, together with, in each case, a one-line description of what is wrong with them. Since there are more Intercessors than there are requests for healing it usually results in each person who asks for prayer being prayed for by ten or so Intercessors. The Intercessors undertake to pray for their five people daily until they receive the next set of names.

Personally, I find intercession difficult. Often, indeed, we discourage people from becoming Intercessors. We don't want people sending their names in unless they feel that the Lord really has called them to this work. It is a real commitment to pray for these five people every day, and in addition, to pray daily for all of us who work here at the Mission. But we're always thrilled when another person decides to send in their name!

It is important, when praying for somebody who is sick, to see them clearly in the mind's eye, whole and fit and well. Agnes Sanford makes this point in her splendid book, *The Healing Light*, one of the best books written on the healing ministry. She says that if you pray for the person's recovery, but see them sick, there is a sense in which you are pinning their sickness on them.

It is exciting to see the Lord bringing more and more people here who are seeking ministry. After we'd been here a few months, Audrey and I found ourselves running the Mission on our own—apart from one part-time helper handling correspondence, mailing lists etc. It was hard work, but we were able to do it. However, with the growth in the work, that would now be impossible, and under the Lord's leading, we have been building up a team of people who each come in, one or two days a week, and help us with the work; all of them, of course, are dedicated Christians and some of them are active in ministering with us.

There is quite a lot of telephone ministry. People ring up with problems, and whilst they seldom ask for prayer over the telephone, they invariably seem pleased when we offer to pray with them. Indeed, we have had some lovely answers to telephoned prayer. One of the team who was answering the telephone typed out the following note a few weeks ago:

Last week a lady rang us in distress. She was taking too many pills, she said, the house was getting her down, and she couldn't keep off the drink. We prayed with her over the telephone.

She rang today full of joy and peace. Her drinking problem had completely gone, and she was 'living in the Lord'. She had thrown her pills away (sleeping pills and slimming pills), and she felt that she had been having a week of revelation. She sounded a completely different person. She had overcome her fetish about constantly cleaning the house, and she now consulted the Lord about everything she did. She was overjoyed.

One is tempted to say: 'Thank God for the telephone.'

Most of the basement of 20 Dawson Place has been converted into a lovely chapel, and the two weekly 'Healing Services' are held here. But increasingly I hesitate to call them 'Healing Services', as this seems to give the wrong emphasis. They are essentially times of worship, when the thirty or forty people who may be there join together in joyful praise of their loving Lord. We have found that it is when people seek the Lord for His own sake—for what they can give to Him—that He blesses so richly. I prefer to think of our services as being 'times of worship, at which people get healed'. At the end of each service four or five of the team (including Audrey and me) will be ministering with the laying on of hands and anyone can come up to any of us for ten or fifteen minutes of individual counselling and prayer. Thus, it may be two to three hours from when the service starts to when the last person leaves. But we always give those who aren't seeking ministry, the chance to leave before the ministry starts.

The Mission, however, is not a church, and, partly to emphasise this point it is shut at weekends. We would never want to draw people away from their own churches. But part of the reason, too, is to give the Missioner—and in our case, his wife, too—the opportunity to accept invitations to share with others what the Lord has been teaching us. This may involve preaching in a church or fellowship in London, or it may involve travelling anywhere in England, (or at times even overseas) to speak on the healing ministry, to conduct seminars and indeed to minister ourselves at Healing Services: these more distant engagements often take up the whole weekend.

But the main work is individual ministry at the Mission, work in which the other members of the team play a gradually increasing part.

Audrey and I enjoy ministering together, and we think the ideal is always to have a man and a woman, backing each other up with prayer. Often, it seems that the woman is given more discernment, and quite often the man is given a better sense of timing. But usually, there simply isn't time for both of us to minister to the same person; Audrey will be with one person, while I'm with another. When we know in advance that it is a case of deliverance, then we always make a point of ministering together.

When someone comes in for ministry, we start by letting them talk. Almost invariably, they have problems which they want to get off their chest. For a few years, Audrey was a member of the Samaritans, that organisation which helps people who are suicidal or at the end of their tether. Her experience there showed her how necessary it was to be a good listener. On one occasion, a man came in to see her. He talked without drawing breath for three-quarters of an hour, over a cup of coffee. He then got up, reached out his hand to her and said, 'Thank you, you've been extremely helpful'. Audrey had not said a word.

At this stage, while they are talking, one must always try and be receptive to what the Lord, Himself, may be saying to us, and often He gives us a word to this effect or that, and we are able to help. However, almost invariably, the time comes after half an hour or so, when one just senses that to go on talking any longer would be a waste of time. So we say—'Let's pray!'

J came to see me the other day. She is in her mid-forties and she'd suffered much depression when she was growing up; as a result she has had many emotional problems. She told me that she had been having counselling for many months with a well-known counselling service; 'They've definitely helped me', she said, adding, 'but now I have come to be healed'. Consequently, we got straight down to prayer—and she received much healing. Her experience illustrates how the Lord can work both through the guidance of the counsellor, and through the healing prayer of those He calls to this ministry.

We normally pray for people standing up. We see our ministry as helping the person to receive the healing love of Jesus. Certainly, we make it abundantly clear that we have no power to heal, ourselves. I think part of the ministry consists of helping the person to see the Lord in their mind, and in helping them to open their heart to receive His forgiveness, His love and His healing. Consequently, we make a point of never standing in front of somebody as we minister to them. It is easier for the person to picture Jesus in front of them, with us simply on the sidelines.

So often people think that, for their prayer to be answered, they have to be very 'good' prayers; they think that one must be very 'expert' in praying. This attitude is completely false. What matters is that the Lord loves us, and He is always waiting for us to accept Him, to invite Him into our hearts, and let Him do His wonderful work within us. He longs to take the initiative if only we will let Him. Our part in many ways is just to be passive, and to receive Him.

Once a person can accept the love of Jesus, they are on the road to being healed. Audrey quotes a doctor, who once said,

'I've been prescribing medicines for years. Some work, and some don't. But there is one prescription for all patients which always works, and that is love.' A questioner asked him, 'What if it doesn't work?' The doctor replied, 'Then double the dose.' At the Healing Mission, we see our role as being to minister the love of Jesus to those who come to us.

We normally minister with me on the left hand side, and Audrey, if she is there, on the right hand side of the person we are ministering to. We may lead them through a prayer of repentance. We certainly lead them to renounce anything of the occult if they have been involved in this. We may lead them to recommit their lives completely to the Lord. Then we just pray that the Lord will release His healing love upon them, and make them whole in spirit, soul and body. But it is very much a question of following the inner prompting of the Holy Spirit. I don't think we ever pray the same for any two people. For ourselves, we find the gift of praying in tongues is invaluable. So often we simply don't know what to pray; we then pray in tongues, and sometimes the English words, or sometimes a picture or a Bible verse comes into one of our minds. But although this gift is an integral part of our own ministry, clearly there are others whom the Lord leads in prayer without the use of tongues. What is vital is to be praying as He leads. Indeed one goes on praying until one senses that one has prayed through what is necessary.

Quite often, the person we are praying for, falls backwards to the ground under the power of the Holy Spirit. Being quite tall, I have no difficulty in catching people as they fall and lowering them gently to the hearth rug, where they can rest their head upon a cushion. It is less easy for Audrey when she is alone, as she is not particularly tall, but she normally ministers upstairs in the sitting room, where there is a couch. There are those who are involved in this ministry who regard this as a lack of faith! They assert—and it may be true—that if under the power of the Holy Spirit, somebody falls backwards to the ground, they are in His hands and they won't hurt themselves. I'm afraid that my level of faith is not sufficient to let them fall without gently catching them under the armpits!

We have seen the Holy Spirit falling powerfully on people as they stood upright, and we simply don't know why some people fall and some don't. Audrey, herself, has only fallen once under the power of the Holy Spirit. When I fell, I could easily have resisted the gentle impulse. But I would, then, have missed a very precious experience; as I lay on the floor then I was gloriously aware of being with Jesus. What we always say to people as we minister to them is that if they feel that they are going backwards, it seems silly to resist. After all, the point of our praying with them is to help them to open up and to receive the healing love of the Lord, and if they are going to resist the impulse to fall, they may block His healing love if He wants to exercise it in that way.

I remember the first time this happened while I was praying with someone. I was praying with a girl, and hadn't yet learnt to keep my eyes open when I prayed; when I opened them, great was my surprise when I found that she was no longer there, but on the floor in a heap at my feet. But normally people fall backwards.

We don't understand what happens when people fall under the power of the Spirit, except to say that it seems to be a deep release—a time when the Lord, Himself, ministers to them at a very deep level. I think of one person who was healed of epilepsy as she fell. I can think of various people from whom it was fairly clear that unclean spirits were coming out as they felt the power of the Holy Spirit. My mind goes back to R. She was in her fifties, and she had been rejected all her life. Her parents despised her and rejected her. Her husband despised and rejected her, and now her son despised and rejected her. As we ministered to her, we talked to her about the love of the Lord for her, but she interrupted impatiently; 'I know all that,' she said, 'I go to church every Sunday. I can accept intellectually that He loves me, but the trouble is, I just don't feel it in my heart.' We prayed for the power of the Holy Spirit to fall on R, and she fell backwards. Often, as the Holy Spirit works upon somebody, one sees a very quick fluttering of the eyelids. When she opened her eyes, we asked her what had been happening. She said, 'I

104

actually felt the power of the Holy Spirit on me. Now I *know* that Jesus loves me, because I have felt the power of His love.' We felt the Lord had achieved His purpose in bring R here.

Another girl I remember praying for in this way was J. J was in her early thirties, her face drawn, and no happiness in her expression. She had had an unhappy childhood. Her father had been demanding, and she, too, couldn't really take in that Jesus loved her. I asked if she had committed her life to Him, and she said, well actually she hadn't. She was afraid if she committed her life to Him, He would want her to do something terrible. I tried to show her that Jesus really loved her, but she couldn't or wouldn't take it in. We then stood up, I prayed for the power of the Holy Spirit to fall upon her, and she fell; one could see from the relaxation of her body, and from the fluttering of her eyelids that the Holy Spirit was working fairly powerfully in her. When she opened her eyes and sat up, I asked her what Jesus had been saying to her. A lovely smile came over her face as she said, 'Jesus wants me to be happy.'

A young man came from Wales, a perfectly normal young man of about thirty, married, with a happy home, children and a job. As I prayed he fell in the power of the Holy Spirit, and again one could see the Holy Spirit working quite powerfully in him. As he got up he said, 'I think that was the most wonderful experience of my whole life.' We praise God for the way He ministers to His children.

A was healed of her epilepsy when she fell under the power of the Holy Spirit. Virginia's healing was as dramatic but took longer. She came to see Audrey in October 1983, aged 39, and having suffered from manic depression from the age of thirteen. She came half a dozen times that autumn. Each time she fell under the power of the Holy Spirit almost before Audrey had prayed for her! She was completely clear by Christmas and has had no recurrence. Indeed she is a valued member of our team at the Mission now.

In Mark chapter 9[36] there is an account of Jesus healing a boy who seems to have fallen to the ground in the same way, while St John tells us that the Temple guard whén they met Jesus in Gethsemane, 'fell to the ground'.[37]

Some people suggest that when people sit up after receiving this kind of ministry, one should say to them 'What are you feeling?' We are doubtful if this is the right question. If somebody asks me what I'm feeling, my thoughts turn inwards to myself, and as they turn inward, they turn away from the Lord. We think the better question is to ask, 'What do you think the Lord has been saying to you?' Then one's thoughts turn outwards to Him.

But then I think of B. B is in his sixties, he lives in the Midlands, and he came to us for prayer as he had cancer of his lung. There was no question of his falling; he never even swayed. But he was very aware of the power of the Holy Spirit upon him as we prayed, and indeed I remember his turning to me with the comment, 'Pretty powerful, that was!' He was completely healed within three months. We just don't know why some people feel that gentle pressure on their chest, pushing them backwards, and some don't.

Many people come to us who are lonely and indeed loneliness is one of the curses of the present day. There are so many old people living alone, who are thrown back on their own resources through lack of company. But loneliness not only affects the elderly; many young people leave home to set out into the world, and then find themselves living alone in a bed-sitting room. Loneliness afflicts people of all ages.

Some months ago, Audrey and I were ministering to a girl in her late twenties, who had had a horrifying childhood. She was an only child, who had lived alone with her mother (she had never known her father). Her mother was an alcoholic, and was promiscuous, and you can imagine what it was like for a sensitive young girl growing up alone in that atmosphere. She ran away from home at the age of fourteen, because she couldn't stand it any longer. She told us that the only way she had managed to keep going until then, was because she had a little friend. 'I used to tell my little friend everything,' she said. One could imagine her as a small girl pouring out all her problems, her sorrows and her fears to her little friend. Then she looked up at us. 'My little friend was Jesus,' she said.

If we are lonely, we need to get into the way of chatting to Jesus (or our Heavenly Father) like this girl chatted to her 'little friend'. We can tell Him all about our worries and our fears. The trouble with being alone a lot, is that it makes us turn inwards to ourselves. We tend to shut ourselves in 'the little dark dungeon of self', as Luther called it. If we can learn to chat to Jesus, and share all our thoughts with Him, then imperceptibly we find ourselves turning outwards from ourselves to Him. A little book called *The Practice of the Presence of God*, tells how Brother Lawrence, a lay brother in a medieval French monastery, and who worked there in the scullery, learned to live his whole life in the presence of his loving Father.

We need to train ourselves to live through each day remembering that we are in the presence of the One who is infinite love. We need to keep asking ourselves what we can do which will bring Him joy and will glorify Him. We need to try and 'coax' ourselves, so that we live for Him, giving ourselves to Him and enjoying what will give Him joy. We can learn to discuss with Him the thoughts which come into our minds. If we are alone, anyhow, what matter if we sound as if we're talking to ourselves!

Another course which brings joy in heaven, is to count our blessings. We had a letter from a young mother, who wrote that each night she and her two small children count their blessings on their fingers, a quick thank-you prayer to Jesus for each of their ten fingers. This is a lovely practice for little children—and since Jesus said we must all be as little children, to enter the kingdom of heaven,[38] it is just as useful for those of us who are grown up or elderly.

Again it has been said that the best cure for loneliness is to pray for other people. As we pray for them, so again our thoughts turn outward from ourselves. Moreover, we can carry on praying for other people throughout the day, sending up little 'arrow' prayers on behalf of complete strangers, and remembering that probably they have had

107

nobody to pray for them that day. A woman walks towards us on the pavement looking tired, 'Lord, lift her up and give her your strength,' we pray. A young man approaches with his girlfriend, 'Lord bless those two. You love them both; keep them free from temptation,' we pray on. A man passes by, looking drawn and worried, 'Lord you love that man. Fill his heart with your peace and assurance.' So we continue to pray. As we wait at the checkout of the supermarket, we can pray for the girl there; very likely no one has prayed for her for the last week. As we pray for her, we bring joy to the heart of the Lord, and we pray down His blessing upon her—and we remember that it is in blessing that we ourselves are blessed.

But, perhaps more than anything, if we live alone and if we have been given this gift, we can continually praise the Lord in tongues. Praying in tongues is the only way I know of obeying Paul's injunction: 'pray without ceasing'.[39]

As we look back over our ministry, we find that a thread which is common to many people is their difficulty in claiming the victory of Jesus. So many people come to us who, whether through hurt or lack of faith, are negative in their thinking and in their lives; they may be aware that they are missing out on the joy, the peace and the fulfilment of a life truly committed to Jesus, and usually they don't know how to achieve that.

We need to remember some of the sure promises that we have been given. For instance, Paul wrote robustly to Timothy (2 Timothy 1:7): 'God did not give us a spirit of timidity, but a spirit of power, of love and of self-discipline', and He reminds Timothy to fan into flame that gift of God which was in him through the laying on of hands. One of my favourite quotations is from Paul's letter to the Corinthians: 'Thanks be to God! He gives us the victory through our Lord Jesus Christ!' (1 Corinthians 15:57)

But how can we put this into practice; how can we help people to change from a negative and, indeed, often defeatist attitude to one of confidence, joy and fulfilment?

108

With this in mind, fairly early on in our time at the Mission, we put together some notes which we entitled *Living in Victory*. You will find these notes, together with the lovely illustrations by Diane Matthes, as an appendix at the end of this book.

# 11

# Healing of Memories and the Cross

Many people who come to us for help at the Healing Mission have suffered emotional hurt earlier in their lives, and although suppressed, this has not yet been healed. Sometimes if someone has suffered much hurt we lead them to the cross. We see them as a child and we lead them by the hand to where Jesus is hanging on the cross. It can then be a matter of painting a word picture of Him as He hangs there. Not only does this serve to introduce the person to a new aspect of Jesus, but it also helps them to take their mind off their problems and to turn outwards to Him.

One can lead them round to the view of the cross which is never painted. As one stands with them to one side and sees Jesus' body hanging forward somewhat from the wooden cross, we can see that His back is torn to shreds, from the neck to the knees. That was what happened at a Roman flogging such as He had just suffered. Sharpened nails were embedded in the leather thongs with the intent to rip the skin and then the flesh off the naked back of the victim. Men often went mad under the pain of a Roman flogging. As we stand with the person beside Jesus, we see His back as a mass of torn, living human flesh, in some places with the blood clotted, in other places still bleeding, and with black flies crawling all over the living flesh, under the heat of the Middle Eastern sun.

The feeling of horror within us grows as we move round to the front and see the nails, probably driven through the wrists rather than the hands, as the flesh of the hands would have torn under the weight of His body. We see the nails driven through his feet. We see the black rings under His eyes, and then, once again, we become aware of the incredible self control as we hear His voice calling out, calm and steady, despite the physical torture and despite the fact that Satan was being allowed to throw everything he had at Him in order to break Him. The horror changes to wonder and amazement as we hear him call out to John asking him to take care of His mother.[40]

We realise then that so many pictures of the Crucifixion miss the point. The Crucifixion was an enormous victory, once and for all, over the forces of sin and darkness. Satan did everything he could to break Jesus, and Jesus won. Down the centuries, one can still hear echoing that last great cry of triumph from the cross, 'It is accomplished!' It was the same word that was used when a commercial debt had been paid in full.

At that moment Jesus knew that he had broken the power of evil in this world once and for all. He had achieved the purpose for which He came into this world and, as we read in the gospel story, He then bowed His head, gave up His spirit deliberately, and died.

As we stand there with the person we are ministering to, we see Jesus, as it were, coming down from the cross—Jesus now in all the glory of the resurrection, resplendent in light and in power. As we stand there and worship Him, it is so natural to say to the person to whom we are ministering, 'Put your right hand now into your heart; put it right into your heart and take out all the pain, all the hurt and all the sadness which is there. Take it out and see it, a nasty black mess on your right hand, and hand it over to Jesus.' They will tell you that they see Jesus taking it from them. They will tell you that as He holds it—perhaps he holds the blackness against His own heart—all the sorrow and the sadness melts away and a few drops of pure water fall to the ground.

And very often the remark is made, 'I actually felt the pain and the sadness leave me.'

I remember a woman called J coming to see me. She

was about fifty. I forget what her particular problem was, but I spent an hour and a half with her and had the impression that whatever the problem was, it had been solved. I suggested that she might like a brief communion service before leaving, and she agreed with enthusiasm. When two or three of us are together, sharing in a little informal communion service, we often do it, as it were, meditatively, and without the book of words. On this occasion, we had each already confessed where we stood before the Lord. We had accepted our sinfulness, we had accepted our need for Him, and we had accepted His forgiveness. I then felt we could move straight on to the actual celebration of communion. I led J to see, in her mind's eye, that we were sitting at the end of the table in that upper room, at that meal which the world has since come to know as the Last Supper.[41] Judas had already left the room, and we saw, as he opened the door, that dark had already fallen. There were eleven disciples left. Perhaps Jesus was at the far end of the table, looking down towards us. We pictured John, the beloved disciple, beside him and the other disciples on either side of the table. We felt the sense of awe, and perhaps of expectancy. That extraordinary young Man, whom the disciples had given up everything to follow for the last two or three years, had surprised them yet again, when a few minutes earlier, He had taken off all his clothes, except for His loin cloth, and taking upon Himself the role of the meanest slave, had deliberately gone round washing the feet of each one of them. Peter's rebuke was still ringing in their ears, as was Jesus' reply.[42] A silence had descended on the men in that upper room, and the disciples must have sensed somehow that tremendous happenings were about to take place.

Jesus must have known that in a few minutes time, He would Himself be going out into the night for that last agonising prayer in the Garden of Gethsemane, when He would be praying to His Heavenly Father, asking if there was any way He could be spared the torture which other wise lay ahead of Him. And in His heart He must have known that as

He was to pray 'Thy will be done', so there would be no alternative. He must have imagined the appalling torture of a Roman flogging, the pain of crucifixion, and even worse than these, the loneliness as the full weight of Satan's power was unleashed upon Him. And yet, as in our imagination we pictured ourselves sitting and looking up the table to Jesus, we saw Him, as always, completely relaxed, and in control of the situation. As we looked into His eyes we saw the suffering, the love and the yearning as He longed to have our whole hearts surrendered to Him. Then it seemed that imperceptibly the Holy Spirit took over.

'I see Jesus beckoning to you', I said to J. 'I see you as a little child of seven, getting up and walking round the table to Jesus. No', I said, 'you're not walking, you're running. You're running to Jesus, and I can see you jumping, jumping on to His lap, and I can see you giggling with sheer joy as you, a little child of seven, snuggle in Jesus' arms. You look so gloriously happy there, blissfully happy, as you feel secure with His strong left arm round your shoulders, and as you lean back on His chest, you feel the warmth of His body, you can feel His heart beating. you look up into His smiling face, you feel the warmth of His love, you feel His breath upon your face only a few inches above your own, and you're just transported into utter joy.' Then after a little while I said, 'I see you getting down, and walking back to the end of the table.'

Then we went on, as we have done many times before and since, and together we saw Jesus taking the bread, blessing it, breaking it, and giving it to His disciples. As we spoke the words of consecration, we blessed the two small wafers which were on the table in front of us. Similarly, we saw Him take the wine, give thanks and bless it, and we repeated the words of consecration, as we blessed the wine in His name and so we shared in His Body and His Blood.

When it was over, J thanked me and said it had been a very meaningful little service of Communion—and then she added, 'Of course, rejection has always been my trouble.' I was horrified when I heard that. Had I now been two hours with this woman, and had I totally failed to grasp the point, I wondered. Something of my concern was expressed in what I said to her. 'No,' she said, 'it's all right, I've now been healed from the rejection. But you got my age wrong.'

I was completely baffled, and I asked her what on earth she meant. J explained. She said that her mother had died when she was six, and her father had married again. She said the memory that had always really hurt her, was the memory of when she had run to her father and thrown herself into his arms, and her step-mother had said, 'No, J, you are too old a girl now to be hugged by your father.' Her father had let her go. 'Never again did I feel the warmth and the security of my father hugging me,' she said. 'But', she added, 'I've been healed in the last few minutes, only you got my age wrong. You said I was a little girl of seven. I was eight, when my father rejected me. But as you were painting that picture, God healed me of that hurt from over forty years ago.'

It is lovely how, if one is really following where the Holy Spirit is leading, He will just take over. I think only once since then have I felt it right to lead somebody to clamber up on Jesus's knee at the Last Supper in the same way, and I don't believe it worked then. I believe I was trying to make it work in my own strength, and not following the Holy Spirit.

Many books have been written recently about healing people's memories. It is true that many of us carry around for years the memories of deep hurts which were too grave for us to handle at the time and which we therefore thrust down into our unconscious minds. These hurts need healing. But one cannot 'switch on' the healing of memories. One can lead someone to experience again the hurt of many years ago and one can then introduce Jesus into the situation, with His compassion and His love. But the healing only comes as we allow the Holy Spirit to lead us, and to have His gentle way. I know that, for myself, I have had much inner healing from the Holy Spirit, and quite a lot of it since we have been at the Mission.

I remember a lovely story that B told me about Jesus on the cross. B is a man of about my age. Life has been hard for him.

114

His wife left him and she has custody of the children. B has next to no money, and what money there is goes on the children's education. B lives alone in a tiny bed-sitting-room somewhere in the East End of London. For his part, he loves his children, he still loves his wife, and he has found the change in his lifestyle very hard to take. One night he told me he was particularly depressed, and he just committed himself briefly to the Lord, before drifting off to sleep. He woke up in the middle of the night really feeling the full weight of depression. He sat up in bed, and as he wrestled with the depression, he looked above him. He looked at the crucifix hanging above his bed, and light was shining on it. As he looked at the crucifix, at that little image of Jesus hanging on the cross, he forgot his own pain and his sorrows, and a lovely peace came over him. He lay down and slept quietly and serenely until the morning.

When he woke up in the morning, he puzzled over the light which had shone on the crucifix. His first thought was that he had forgotten to draw the curtains properly. But no, he looked; the curtains were heavy, dark curtains, and they were drawn completely across the window. He then wondered if perhaps after all he hadn't drawn them properly, but somehow, after seeing the crucifix, had got up in his sleep, and drawn them. Perhaps it was the light from one of the street lights outside, which had come through a chink in the curtains and shone on the crucifix. He got up and examined the position of those lights that he could see from his window. He then realised that it was impossible, owing to their position, for any of them to have cast their light on the crucifix. At that, he just knelt down and thanked the Lord for this lovely little miracle, that He, in His love and compassion, had purposely illuminated His crucifix to bring comfort and peace to B's heart.

The cross must always be a mystery to us. Certainly, I know that I don't begin to understand fully what happened on the cross. I do know that a lot of people, particularly those who have really been blessed with the Holy Spirit, are aware of a very personal relationship with Jesus on the cross.

Common sense tells us that as He died on the cross, He was dying for the sake of millions upon millions of people who have lived in this world, and for many millions more people who are living in this world now. Yet, people often tell me that they are aware of a very real sense in which Jesus actually gave himself on the cross, personally, for them.

I have always thought that this was a lovely thing to be aware of, but until recently, I have never been able to get over the feeling that I was just one of many, many millions for whom He died. However, as we allow ourselves to be open to the Holy Spirit, in a wonderful way He does lead us into the truth,[43] and I think it is only in the last few weeks that I have begun to be aware that Jesus actually died personally for me. In His love he wanted me to be free, to be forgiven, and to be healed. Somehow, of recent weeks the cross has begun to be for me something intensely personal, an expression of the perfect love of God, as revealed in Jesus, just for me.

Many people find it difficult to reconcile the cross with a God of love. If God is perfect love, they say, why should He want to sacrifice His Son? Why should He want His Son to endure such an appalling death? Indeed, was it just to satisfy His own ego? I have much sympathy with people who make remarks like this. However, I think we have to remember, firstly, that the love of God the Father for God the Son is so great and so divine that God was actually dying Himself in the form of His Son upon the cross, that God the Father was suffering all the physical agony of torture and of spiritual separation from Him, which Jesus suffered as He hung upon the cross.

I think, too, we need to remember, that besides being a God of love, besides being a God of perfect holiness, He is also a God of perfect justice. Justice requires that punishment follows a crime. Somehow, as we saw earlier, at the time of the fall, mankind said to himself, 'We know what God wants. We know what God has told us. We don't care! We are following what we want to do.' Man sinned; man set himself up against God; man cut himself off from the love of

God. That was, if you like, the crime. Somehow, the perfect justice of a God who is perfect in every way required that the crime should be followed by due punishment. But then, because God is perfect love, as well as being perfect justice, He paid the price for us Himself upon the cross.

There is a story, which illustrates these two aspects of God's nature, His perfect love and His perfect justice. The story goes like this. Once there was a man who committed some great crime against the law of the land. He knew that he was guilty. He had no chance of getting off. As he lay in prison, awaiting the time of his trial, he learnt the name of the judge who was to try him. He told his cell-mates and they groaned. 'You won't have any mercy from old so-and-so,' they said. 'That judge is absolutely fair, but he won't let you off any part of the punishment for what you have done.'

The time came for the trial. The evidence was heard. The jury pronounced the man guilty—which he was—and the judge pronounced the sentence. The prisoner returned to his cell, with the words of the sentence ringing in his ears. The judge had sentenced him to an enormous fine which he couldn't possibly pay, or alternatively to a long period of years in prison. He had to admit, as he reflected, that the judge had been fair, and that he deserved the full sentence which he had been given. As he was locked up alone again in the cell, he held his head in his hands in despair at the thought of the years in prison which lay ahead of him.

Then he heard the key turn in the lock. He looked up, and to his surprise, he saw the judge come into the cell, this time not in his judicial robes but wearing ordinary clothes. The judge quietly walked over to him, took an envelope out of his pocket, put it into the prisoner's hands and said 'I think this will help you'. He went out of the door; the prisoner heard the key turn in the lock again, and he was left alone once more.

It was a few minutes before he thought that perhaps he might as well look at the envelope which the judge had put into his hands. He opened it, and saw a cheque made out on the judge's own personal bank account, for the full amount of the fine. Now I'm not telling that story as being true. I can't believe that it is true. But I think that that story, if it were true, would illustrate something of how justice and love are combined in the nature of the God who is perfect in every way.

But the story doesn't end there. Of what use to the prisoner was a cheque in his hands? Of itself, that cheque was worth nothing, it was just a small piece of paper with some writing on. In order to turn that cheque into money with which he could pay the fine, the prisoner had to do something himself. He had to endorse that cheque, and he had to arrange for someone to present it to a bank, and cash it. Then with the cash which the cheque realised, he would be able to pay his fine and go free.

Jesus has paid the price of my sins, and yours, on the cross. He died, in order that we should be forgiven, that we should be free, and that we should be healed. But that is of no good to us unless we accept what He has done for us. We can accept it in our heads, but often we find it hard to accept it in our hearts.

Somebody once said that the longest journey in the world is represented by those twelve inches from our heads to our hearts. The most practical way I know of helping our unconscious mind to receive an eternal and spiritual truth, is to thank the Lord for it. If you can accept in your head that Jesus died once and for all on the cross to set us free from our sins,[44] and to heal us in every sense,[45] but are finding it difficult to believe that truth in your heart, then thank Him for it. When you thank Him for it, don't just wait until you feel like thanking Him; that feeling will probably never come. Thank Him as a matter of discipline, keep thanking Him; thank Him perhaps a hundred times a day, whether you feel like it or not, just a simple prayer of thanks; 'Thank you Jesus, that in your divine love, you gave yourself on the cross so that I might be forgiven, freed and made whole.' Each time you thank Him, you are stepping out in faith, believing that what the Bible says is, in fact, the truth.

If we try repeating a statement which is not true,

something silly like, 'Thank you Lord for making daffodils blue with pink spots,' then our unconscious minds will reject that statement. However, the Lord made us so that if we thank Him for something in His truth, then our unconscious minds will come to accept that truth. Then we come to believe deep in our hearts what hitherto we have been praying as a matter of will. Then the day will come, perhaps before very long, when we find ourselves thanking the Lord for what He did for us on the cross, no longer as a matter of mental discipline but genuinely thanking Him from the heart.

I remember a girl called S, who came for ministry. She was about twenty-nine, and had had an appalling history of rejection in her childhood. I can't remember why, but at the age of fourteen, her mother had told her that she was to leave home; she could live in the caravan at the end of the garden. Her mother said she would put out a bucket of cold water on the kitchen doorstep each day, and that was to be the only contact of any sort which, at the age of fourteen, she was to have with her home or her family. I remember asking S how she existed, how she managed to get food, how she cooked it, how she kept herself warm during the cold winter, indeed how she kept herself alive. She replied that she had no idea, but somehow she had survived. Small wonder was it then, that when she came to us, although she could accept in her head that Jesus loved her, she found it impossible to believe in her heart that He could love her. The pain of rejection was too deep.

Under different circumstances, the Holy Spirit might have led us so that she could have seen Jesus with her in that caravan. She could have relived that rejection of those teenage years, and she could have felt, in place of that rejection, the comfort of knowing that Jesus with His love and His security, had been with her all the time. She could have re-lived the fear and the pain of putting herself to bed at the age of fourteen in that caravan, all alone, in the knowledge which she knew now, that Jesus had been there with her.

119

But on this occasion, He led differently. As S was going, I said to her, 'S, will you just lift your eyes to the Lord, perhaps a hundred times a day, for the next few days, and regardless of your feelings, just pray, 'Thank you, Jesus that you love me. Amen.' S went out of the door, saying that she would.

It must have been about a week later that we had a lovely letter from her, which we have still got, a letter full of joy. In her letter she said that it had taken two days of praying like that, and then her unconscious mind had begun to accept the reality of Jesus' love for her. Since then things had improved, and in every respect had begun to be different. She had been able to pray again, and she had begun to accept His love for the first time in fifteen years.

So often we keep asking for the same thing. Night after night, we keep asking: Lord, please do this or that, please help me in this or that way. So often, as we repeat that prayer, in effect all we are saying is, 'Lord perhaps you weren't really listening when I prayed last night, I'd better pray again tonight, to make sure you really hear.' If only on those occasions we would step out in faith! If only we would actually stop asking for whatever it is, and switch over to the prayer of thanks, which is the prayer of faith. If only we would say, 'Thank you, Lord, that in your love for me you heard my prayer last night. Thank you Lord, in faith, that I know that you have got the answer to my prayer in hand. Thank you Lord, that you are a God who answers prayer.'

We may not feel like praying like that, but we need to step out in faith. There is often more power in that simple prayer of thanks than there is in repeating the same request, day after day.

# 12

# Healing the Whole Person

---

When I was working in the City, I learnt fairly soon what seemed a most important lesson, namely that what matters is what works. From time to time I wondered whether I ought to try and prepare myself for perhaps eventually running our Group by taking a course, for instance, in economics. But each time I thought of it, I realised that what was going to matter, if I was going to do my job properly in the City, was not so much the theory, but the practical aspect of how to do it. In the context of the City, I had become a realist.

Then, as my life unfolded and I began to turn increasingly to the Lord, I realised the advantages of applying the same test to one's Christian faith. Was it practical, and did it work? I would commend anyone to apply that test. Curiously enough, and to my surprise, I found that the more I tested the Christian faith with the question: 'Does it work?', the stronger my faith became!

Nonetheless, for a long time, healing was an area in which I had real difficulties. I used to be cynical about healing services. My idea of a healing service, was that people went up to the altar rail on their crutches, with their arms in slings, and wheezing with bronchitis. The vicar then moved down the line, laying hands on each one in turn. They then all trooped back to their seats, still on crutches, their arms still in slings, and still wheezing. And then the vicar spent the rest of the afternoon explaining why nothing had happened. I take a very different view today.

The scriptural basis for the church's healing ministry

seems clear. St Luke tells us that Jesus called the twelve disciples together, 'and gave them power and authority to drive out all demons and to cure diseases, and He sent them out to preach the Kingdom of God, and to heal the sick'.[46] We get the same message in Matthew's gospel: 'As you go preach this message: "the kingdom of heaven is near. Heal the sick, raise the dead, cleanse those who have leprosy, drive out demons".'[47] We read of Jesus giving the same instructions to the seventy as He sent them out.[48] There seems no doubt that the early disciples were instructed by Jesus to go out and heal the sick, and indeed, from the accounts in the book of Acts, it is clear that this is precisely what they went on doing after Jesus had died and risen from the dead.

But there are those who will say, 'Yes, we accept this is what happened during our Lord's lifetime and immediately after His death and resurrection. In order to get the early church established it was necessary for God to give to those early followers, the power to heal the sick. But after the first few decades, and once the church was established, God withdrew that power.'

This argument seems to fall to the ground for three reasons. Firstly, it is not scriptural. At the end of Matthew's Gospel, Jesus says quite clearly, 'All authority in heaven and on earth has been given to me. Therefore go and make disciples of all nations . . . teaching them to obey everything I have commanded you.'[49] It is clear from that passage that Jesus expected all the world to be taught by the disciples and by those who followed them, to obey everything that He had commanded the original disciples to do. It would have been pointless for those who followed the original disciples to have taught that Christians were to heal the sick if God had withdrawn from men the power to do so.

Secondly, if God, in a slightly arbitrary manner, bestowed on the early Christians the power to perform miracles and heal, and then after a few decades decided that enough was enough, and that he would withdraw that power, He would have been inconsistent. If God is really inconsistent, then none of us has a chance of knowing Him. If God is the kind of being who says one thing one day, and something else the next day, we, who seek to follow Him, would simply never know where we were with Him; it would depend entirely upon His mood of the moment. Moreover, that kind of a God would not be perfect. It seems clear to me that a God who is perfect in every way must be consistent and must always be true to His own character.

After all, if one looks at the laws of nature, the laws of medicine, or the laws of science, they all point to a consistency running through God's creation. For example, if the application of a particular trace element to a field has a particular result today, application of the same trace element to a precisely similar field tomorrow, will have the same result. Similarly, in medicine, if the cure for one disease in one person is a particular medicine, a similar person, suffering from precisely the same disease, will be cured by being given the same medicine. There is a thread of consistency running through the whole of nature, and I believe this consistency reflects the character of God. I believe that God, who is perfect, is also perfect in His consistency. Consequently, I find it hard to believe that God would pour out on to His chosen few a particular power, at a particular time in history, and would then arbitrarily withdraw it after a given period. After all, the Lord is the same yesterday, today and for ever.[50]

However, the strongest argument against the claim that the healing miracles only went on for a few decades after our Lord's death, lies quite simply in the fact that that statement is historically untrue. It is quite clear, as one reads the early Fathers, that the early church expected miracles to happen, and saw them happening, until around the middle of the third century. Going back a similar number of years today takes us back to the period, in the eighteenth century, well before the French Revolution, when France was still ruled by a corrupt monarchy. It take us back before the Industrial Revolution in our country. It takes us back to a time when England's population was mainly composed of peasants and agricultural labourers. In other words, the period during which the early church expected to see miracles, and indeed saw them, was a long one.

Most of the time, from the death and resurrection of Jesus to roughly the middle of the third century, the church endured persecution. The intensity of the persecution varied, but Christians suffered much cruelty, many of them being put to death under torture. During that period, you did not become a Christian unless you were absolutely convinced, in your heart, that the Christian faith was true, and that there was no other way you could live your life. During all those years of persecution, there were indeed no half-hearted Christians. If in any way you were half-hearted about your faith you played for safety and kept away.

Then, during the course of the third century, a change came about. The persecution ceased, and it actually became respectable to be a Christian. People started to go to church because it was the done thing. Perhaps they went because they liked the pastor. No longer was there the same degree of commitment in the members of the third century church. No longer did they need the same burning faith, the same absolute certainty of the power of the risen Lord, before they became Christians. Instead, people became Christians because it was socially acceptable. It was with the disappearance of that burning, irrepressible zeal which the church showed under the persecution of the first two centuries and more, that the miracles ceased to be expected, and thus ceased to happen.

However, since the third century, there have from time to time been genuine religious revivals. When that same burning faith has been present, once more, in the Body of Christ, in His church, the miraculous has again been revealed. Indeed, today, where people accept the power of Christ to heal, and are prepared totally to surrender to Him, they are seeing Him at work, miraculously, in the same way.

We ourselves have seen a young man come into the London Healing Mission on crutches, and walk away down the road, carrying his crutches. We have seen ladies healed of

124

cancer of the breast. We have seen an African lady come up for ministry at the end of one of our Thursday evening healing services, and be healed; she had something defective with her pancreas, besides having high blood pressure. We have seen people healed, instantaneously, from addiction to heroin, to alcohol and to cigarettes. We have seen a deaf man healed. A possession which we appreciate is a card certifying that if the bearer is found unconscious in the road, her name is so-and-so, she suffers from epilepsy, and she is on such and such drugs. She was healed during the period of a few minutes two years ago, and she gave us the card when even the doctors admitted that her epilepsy was no more. She had suffered from epilepsy for seven years, was on a high level of medication, and was still having two or three fits a week before that day in October 1983. She has never had another fit. And so one could go on with the list. We see the Lord moving in power, to a greater or lesser degree, almost every day at the London Healing Mission. A few months ago we had nine instantaneous healings in the space of a fortnight.

People sometimes ask us if they should give up going to their doctor and rely entirely on prayer for healing. Our advice is always to continue with medical treatment unless—and this is very rare—a person is convinced in his own mind that the Lord has specifically said He wants to heal him through prayer alone. If a person is convinced that this is what the Lord wants him to do, then, as a Christian, he must be obedient. But leaving such exceptional cases aside, we remember that the Lord invented the laws of medicine, he invented the cures for the illnesses which afflict mankind, and we feel it is wrong to try and restrict Him to healing through spiritual power alone. The natural healing power of the human body can both be aided by medicine and stimulated through the power of prayer!

At the same time one must remember that there are good doctors and less good doctors, as indeed is the case with the members of every profession. Most doctors, too, are often unable to give every patient as much time as they would like. We are hesitant about some psychiatrists, particularly where ECT is involved.

The medical profession today is increasingly seeing the human person as a whole, and indeed the head of the British Medical Association is on record as saying recently, that he believes that healing depends on a harmony of body, soul and spirit. For so many years now, with the advance of medical science, we have tended, as it were, to cut the human body into little bits. If there is something wrong with your teeth, you go to the dentist. If there is something wrong with your eyes, you go to an oculist. But many people in the medical profession today are beginning again to see that the human being is one single whole. I am quite certain that this is how Jesus saw people, and that He sees them this way today.

As people come to us at the London Healing Mission for ministry—and people come here from all over England—we find that we are led to see them as a whole, with body, soul and spirit. The spirit, as we have seen is that part of them which will live on into eternity. By 'soul', I refer to the emotions, the mind, the will and the brain. People sometimes come to us saying that they are seeking healing for this or that which is wrong with their body. But almost invariably, as we seek to follow the prompting of the Holy Spirit, it seems that He leads us to enquire first of all as to inner healing. So often He seems to lead us, first of all, to minister to their soul, and sometimes, then, the physical healing will follow without even being prayed for.

An Indian lady in her late sixties came to Audrey and me for ministry. She had a lump under her tongue, which she said had the doctors baffled, and she wanted the lump healed. As we prayed with this lady, the word 'resentment' came into one of our minds, and we asked whether there was any resentment in her life, was there anyone who had wronged her, and whom she was refusing to forgive. Then it all poured out. Her son had married a girl whom she disapproved of, and she was resentful of that girl having taken him from her. She was resentful in other areas too. She lived in

126

a flat, and the neighbours were difficult. She was bitter about them.

We explained to her gently, that such resentment was not of the Lord. Jesus tells us quite clearly to forgive others in order that we ourselves may be forgiven.[51] In the Lord's prayer itself, we pray 'Forgive us our trespasses, as we forgive them that trespass against us.'[52] We remember Jesus' words, 'Do not judge and you will not be judged.'[53] It is quite clear that it is for us, as Christians, to forgive our fellow men. Resentment and bitterness actually block the healing power of the Lord, which He longs to pour out on us.

The Indian lady listened attentively. She accepted what we were saying, and she prayed a lovely prayer to the Lord, confessing her sin in being resentful, and praying for His forgiveness. She had hardly got to the end of that prayer, when a lovely smile came over her face. She threw her arms in the air with a cry of 'Alleluia!' Audrey and I were puzzled, to put it mildly. We asked what had happened. 'Why the lump's gone!' she cried. So often the physical healing is dependent on the inner healing, in this case repentance.

I believe that every prayer for healing releases some of our Lord's healing power. So often our difficulty is that we see things from the purely human angle, and we are praying with the wrong emphasis. We merely see the physical ailment. God, however, sees things from the viewpoint of eternity, and He can see into the hearts of those He loves so deeply. As Isaiah wrote, ' "As the heavens are higher than the earth, so are my ways higher than your ways," declares the Lord.'[54]

We do well to remember the Lord's purpose for us. The reason for which we have been created, is because the Lord longs to have each one of us with Him in the joy and fulfilment of perfect worship throughout all eternity. A moment's thought shows that we cannot go to heaven until the Lord has finally perfected us. If one reflects on the awesome, and indeed fearsome holiness of a God who is perfect in every way, dazzling and shining in His glorious holiness, we realise that sin simply could not exist in the presence of such a Being. If sin ever came into His presence, it would simply shrivel up and cease to exist. Well was it said, that God cannot look on sin.[55] If He did, it would cease to be.

Another reason which illustrates why we need to be perfect before we can go to Heaven, is that if we went to Heaven in an imperfect state, we would spoil Heaven for all those who are there already. Heaven, surely, is where everything is perfect. It follows, therefore, that if the Lord created us to be with Him, in perfect joy and fulfilment in Heaven, then He must want us to let Him make us perfect. It must be the will of God to perfect His creation in us.

But God does not only want us to have perfect bodies, He wants us to be perfect in every way. He wants us to be perfect in soul and without blemish, He wants us to be perfected, spotless, and clothed with His own perfect nature in our spirits. I believe that every prayer for healing releases a little more of His healing power, towards the time when He has perfected His creation in us. As Paul wrote, 'He who began a good work in you will carry it on to completion'.[56]

Certainly that time will not be during the present life. St Paul, of all people, writing to Timothy, describes himself as the worst of sinners.[57] If one reads the lives of the Saints, one realises that in fact the closer they get to the Lord in their walk with Him in this world, the more they were aware of their own sinfulness. No, the Lord will not complete the process of making us perfect during our lives in this world. That will have to wait for the time when, as Paul writes, after death we shall all be changed in the twinkling of an eye.[58]

# 13

## *Love that Heals—1*

We see the Lord moving in power to a greater or lesser extent almost every day at the London Healing Mission. When we first came here we used to stop and marvel when someone was healed; now we tend just to lift our hearts in thankfulness and praise to the Lord—and move on to the next person.

Every week we share with those who have come to our healing services, short extracts from letters or phone calls we have received since the previous Thursday, from people giving thanks for answered prayer. There are usually a dozen or so. In addition, people may tell us about answers to prayer. Each month those on our mailing list receive a circular letter which includes a short selection of those weekly thanks-givings. Looking back through these it is hard to see any pattern. We know that it is in the nature of a God of perfect love that He longs to perfect us and make us whole, and, as one would expect, the range of healings is indeed wide.

Many people come to us suffering from depression, which can cripple a person and indeed ruin their life. M was one. The first we heard of her was when her son wrote to us, saying that his mother had just come down from Yorkshire and was looking for a psychiatrist in London. He was trying to persuade her to come to the Mission and eventually succeeded.

The first time she came nothing much happened; we learned that she was fifty-four, and that she was no longer married.

The second time, however, there was a period of deep

prayer and M became aware that she had been healed instantaneously, after ten years of acute depression. I remember the telephone conversation when she rang a week later, 'Andy, I've got another problem to consult you about.' I wondered what it could be this time. She explained that she couldn't possibly draw her invalidity benefit now, because she was completely healed, and she wondered how she was going to live without it. In fact, her doctor was wise. He realised that she was healed, but he said that she could go on with her invalidity benefit as she would need quite a period of time to adjust to the fact of being healed.

Two months later she went to see her psychiatrist. She told us that he was 'flabbergasted' at her healing, but what had puzzled him as much as anything was the lack of withdrawal symptoms. She had thrown all her pills away on the evening of her healing, and with the massive dose she had been on, he just could not understand why there had been a complete absence of withdrawal symptoms.

E was much the same age. She was brought to us by her friend one July, and she asked how long we thought it would be before she was healed of her depression which she had suffered for twenty-five years. We answered that if she came regularly we would be surprised if she wasn't healed in three months. In fact, she didn't come regularly, and it was about seven months before she was totally healed. I remember so well the occasion when she came in for prayer and we said, 'What do you want us to pray for today?' A lovely peaceful smile came over E's face and she said, 'I don't need prayer for anything now; I'm fine thanks.' Seeing the complete change in a person is what makes the work here so wonderful. When E first came in, she had been burdened by her depression and was a colourless person. It was lovely to see her, seven months later, with a sparkle in her eyes and a smile which lit up her face.

Sometimes healing can be immediate. We don't know with any particular person how the Lord wants to act, and we must leave it to Him. C came up to one of us at the altar rail for a brief time of prayer at the end of one of our services. He must have been around sixty, and we had never seen him before. Subsequently, he told us that, as he was prayed for, he felt the love of God pouring over him and healing him immediately of the manic depression from which he had suffered for many years. He had thrown all his medication away, and he said that his life since he was healed 'had been completely changed'.

We have mentioned earlier how Virginia was healed of manic depression. She later wrote this for us:

> I went to the London Healing Mission in early November 1983. I didn't go in faith but in desperation. I had been ill for twenty-six years with bouts of manic depression, and it was a Christian friend who finally made me turn to God for help. I am now ashamed to say that my reasoning was, "Well you've tried everything else, so why not give it a go."
>
> On my first visit after I had unburdened my heart to Audrey, and committed my life to God, Andy joined us to pray the Spirit down to heal me. I didn't know what to expect, I didn't know anything about the Holy Spirit. I think even before they had started to pray I had fallen backwards under the power of the Spirit. Andy did catch me, but I gave them a bit of a surprise. On all further visits exactly the same thing happened, and I nicknamed myself their "Fallen Woman"! The first sensation I can remember, lying on the floor, was one of peace, and this was always the first feeling I had when the Spirit had come upon me. Sometimes as Andy and Audrey prayed over me I had pins and needles. Other times I felt as if I was on a scanning machine with electric currents gently running up and down my body, but always the peace came first. After every visit I felt on top of the world and I just got better and better every day.

Virginia must have come half a dozen times for ministry, and her healing was completed after a total of six weeks. She is now a valued member of our team at the mission, and is so radiant that people who didn't know her, before, find it very hard to believe that she has ever suffered from depression!

Part of the problem of depression is that it makes a person turn inwards, thus cutting themselves off from the healing love of Jesus. It is so important when ministering to people, and especially to someone suffering from depression, to help them to turn outwards to the Lord. One of the team wrote the following letter to a lady in her seventies who has suffered from depression for many many years:

Your letter is in front of me and I feel for you in your pain. Yet even as I feel in my heart for you it is not me who hurts but Jesus, Himself; He who knows you through and through.

As you are reading this letter, I want you to imagine Jesus standing in front of you. Close your eyes if it helps, and just imagine Him there. See how He looks at you—with love and understanding. See how He *loves* you!

Under His gaze of love I see the floodgates opening, and your face is awash with tears—tears of bitterness, loneliness and pain—tears built up over all these years.

Now see Him stretch out His hand towards you. Very gently He wipes those tears from your face and with them He wipes away *all* the pain and *all* the suffering. You are surrounded by His love—embraced in His arms and He says to you: "My daughter, I *love* you".

As you are held in those arms, safe and secure, you are bathed in the love of God—the light from His face surrounds you—banishing all darkness—His Spirit flows into you, flooding you with that light, touching and healing the deepest hurts that you have within you. Within those arms you simply rest, absorbing His healing, breathing it in with every breath, responding to it and to His love. And now you find with a thrill in your heart that just as Jesus carries our sadness, so also He thrills to our gladness, feels our joy and delights in our laughter. For now the depression has gone and in its place is the joy of the Lord. A deep gladness that comes not from your own wishing for it, but actually from Him.

"Rejoice with me for I have seen the risen Lord".

His new life is within you. Thank Him and praise Him for it. As you, yourself, said, "truly a miracle".

But people come to us suffering from other mental illnesses too. A is thirty-two. She had been married and divorced before she was twenty, and had been on sleeping pills for twenty years. After the first time of ministry she threw her pills away and, she told us, slept like a baby. She had a recurrence of insomnia, but it didn't last for more than a few weeks and she then resumed sleeping perfectly and without any medication. But her bigger problem was epilepsy. She was healed of this after prayer at the Mission. We don't know enough medically about epilepsy to know one form from another, but she told us that when she went into Charing Cross Hospital for a scan the staff there were baffled. They said they knew without doubt that she had been an epileptic, whereas the person they had before them just simply was not an epileptic.

We have seen improvement in people suffering from schizophrenia and people sometimes come to us with paranoia. F was in his early thirties and had been in and out of mental hospitals since his late teens. The psychiatrists diagnosed his main problem as being paranoia, that horrid affliction when one is certain not only that everyone is staring at one but that they can see right inside and even read one's thoughts. He came here, perhaps half a dozen times for ministry, without anything very apparent happening. Then there came the day when he had to face up to the question, was he going to follow Jesus without hesitation, or was he not? F himself said that he recognised that the Lord was his only hope and he saw that to draw on His strength meant a deep commitment. After pondering the question for a quarter of an hour, he decided to trust Jesus and follow Him.

The following week he had slipped back and again we had to present him with the same choice. He was quicker this time to accept Jesus. He then went on and asked how long we thought it would be before he was finally healed. We thought much would depend on how totally he gave himself to Jesus, but we indicated that perhaps he might be totally healed in a year.

At this he broke down and wept. 'I simply cannot endure this hell any longer!' Then he turned and said. 'Can we please pray?' As we prayed with him, it was apparent from his expression that he was very open to the power of the Spirit. When we finished praying F said he felt he had been healed; we thought so too. We then asked F to think of

133

something which would really fill him with terror. His reply was the thought of walking down Oxford Street with all those crowds. 'But if you've been healed,' we suggested, 'why don't you do just that?' His friend was at the door with a car, and it would be quite easy to drive him to Marble Arch so that he could walk down Oxford Street. And that is precisely what F then did. But we warned him much would depend on his total commitment to Jesus.

As we read back through the messages of thanksgiving from those who have been healed, cancer is something which recurs fairly often. E came to see Audrey when she had been told by her doctors that she had cancer of the breast and would have to have an operation. She was full of fear and anxiety and extremely nervous about the operation.

We felt this fear needed to be dealt with before the healing could take place, and we asked the Lord to remove it and put His peace in its place. We then rebuked the cancer, and felt convinced that the Lord had healed her. She too felt that she was healed when she left. However, when she got home, she rang up to ask whether she should go into hospital and have the mastectomy, or believe for her healing. We said, 'We think the Lord wants you to believe for your healing.' However, her courage failed her, and she went ahead with the operation. The results of the biopsy revealed there was no cancer present, and she need never have had the operation. God had, therefore, healed her despite her lack of assurance. We have had other such healings, in one case actually feeling a large lump in the breast, and it disappearing after prayer. P wrote to us about her daughter, 'Somehow she was healed and is now whole. Four months ago she had an eleventh hour operation for cancer. Another operation was to follow together with laser treatment. Neither is now necessary. I would like to thank your Intercessors for all the prayer she received.'

H had a very bad throat. Cancer was suspected and an operation was likely. Prayer was offered for her. She woke early one morning suddenly clear in her throat. Her doctor was astounded at the great change for the better, and could not account for it medically. A friend wrote to us saying that

H had subsequently arrived at her prayer group saying, 'Oh how He answers prayer! I'm a different person and no operation is needed, and perhaps now not even any treatment is needed.' Her health and joy were apparent.

P was healed of cancer of the lymph gland during ten minutes of prayer at the end of one of our healing services here.

Homosexuality can wreck a man's life. I would go so far as to say that I don't believe that any homosexual is really happy or really fulfilled. Homosexuality may come about through a boy having had a weak father so he had no example of masculinity as he was growing up, or a mother who smothered him with her emotional love, or some man molesting him sexually when he was younger. There are those who say that the homosexual is physically different from the heterosexual, that he cannot change, and that society, therefore, should adjust to accept his homosexuality. We would retort that, as we have seen the Lord healing physical infirmities, so, if there is a physical difference in homosexuals, the Lord is perfectly capable of healing that as well as healing any psychological sickness that is involved. What is clear is that the Lord longs to perfect his creation in each one of us, and no homosexual would claim, I think, that his way of life was perfect.

We usually point out to homosexuals that there are really only two perfect alternatives for any of us as far as the sexual side of our nature is concerned. One is the joy of Christian marriage, and the other is the joy of celibacy. (If the thought of celibacy does not bring a song of joy in the person's heart, then it is probably not what the Lord has prepared for that person. We have had a few people come to see us who were genuinely called to celibacy, but not many.)

Agnes Sanford likens homosexuality to a river where the natural watercourse has become blocked so that the river bursts its banks and in due course gouges out an alternative channel for itself. She advises praying for the natural course of the emotions to open up again and for alternatives to be blocked. One can say this and more as one is counselling a homosexual, but as always, the power of healing comes through in prayer. After we had prayed for one homosexual, he wrote to us:

All praise and thanks to God. Since coming to you last, most of the old thought patterns have disappeared and I have felt no strong desire to re-establish my old way of life. What a miraculous change.

Perhaps one of the saddest interviews I have ever had was with a nineteen-year-old homosexual. The man he was living with had come to see me first and he was receptive to what I was saying, and I believe that the Lord had begun to heal him. When his young partner came to see me, the boy told me how he longed to be normal, to marry and have children and to be like other men. I asked him what he was expecting to happen when we started praying for him to be freed from his homosexual tendencies. I remember the empty look on his face as he said, 'I'm expecting nothing.' Sadly, when people expect nothing from prayer, then nothing often happens. Neither he, nor his older friend ever came back.

But one cannot write for long about the Lord healing through the power of prayer without coming to the question of faith. T was twelve years old when his parents brought him to one of our Healing Services. He suffered from paroxysmal coughing. He came up to the altar rail and we asked him what he thought was going to happen. The answer came back with the simple faith of a child, 'Why, Jesus is going to heal me, of course!' He was healed instantaneously. T's father, who is not a believer, wrote to us afterwards, 'We are so grateful. T's paroxysmal coughing fits stopped just like that at your prayer meeting when he said he was cured. Pretty remarkable.'

C, aged two, was too young to believe or indeed to understand what was happening. He was brought to us for prayer by his mother and two or three other friends of hers who had been praying regularly for him. He had been born with various physical defects, one of which was a complete inability to swallow. All his short life he had been fed through a tube. The ladies who brought him had a lovely faith, and they wrote afterwards to say that for the first time he was able to feed normally.

Although it is true that always in the Bible the Lord was looking for faith and the same is true today, yet at the same time, it is not necessary for there to be any particularly 'religious' atmosphere when one prays for a person. I can remember praying for a handicapped child, and as so often happens with such children, her mother spoilt her terribly. Audrey took her mother into another room and prayed with her, and left me with the child. All the time I was praying she was banging round the room, throwing things about and obviously furious at being thwarted in her desire to get back to her mother. It was hardly the atmosphere for prayer! I forget what the particular thing was, for which her mother had brought her, but she told us subsequently that there had been a definite change for the better after I had prayed with the child.

What saddened me, though, was that the mother did not bring the child back for further prayer. I am quite certain that it cannot be the Lord's will that that child should grow up unable to lead a normal life. It must be His will to heal her. And since there was the occasion when Jesus, Himself, had to lay hands on a blind man twice before he was healed, I have no qualms about praying many times for the same person for the same thing! As a matter of sheer common sense it seems to me that if somebody is seen to respond, even to a limited extent, to prayer for healing, then surely they will return for more of the same thing!

An infirmity which is both painful and connected to a person's mental state is arthritis. Quite often there will be a connection between a person being resentful or bitter about something in their life, and the onset of arthritis. It is by no means invariably the case, but it follows quite often.

When we were visiting a parish in Gloucestershire, Audrey ministered to E with the vicar's wife. E was crippled with arthritis, so much so, that once she had sat down, she dreaded getting up. Audrey and the vicar's wife had to support her as she got out of her chair to go into the other room for ministry. Having got there, she said, 'Do you mind if I stay standing because I cannot go through the pain of sitting down and trying to get up again?'

Audrey told her to shut her eyes and concentrate on Jesus, 'Look at Him, whether you picture Him as a man or as light or however you see Him; tell Him you give yourself completely to Him and ask Him to heal you,' Audrey said. This she did, and Audrey continued in prayer. At the end of fifteen or twenty minutes, E opened her eyes and thanked the Lord for touching her. She said she felt the warmth of His healing power go right through her body. She walked unaided into the next room, and said simply, 'I'm healed'. The last Audrey saw of her was when she had joined the others who were waiting in another room, and she was, as Audrey put it, like a yoyo, sitting down and standing up, overcome with wonder that she was now free from the arthritic pain, and showing off to everyone! Small wonder that the friend who brought her wrote to us a week later saying, 'She is a different person'.

It is always a mystery why in some cases the Lord heals instantaneously, and in other people the healing is slower. J wrote to us:

I came to the Healing Mission on April 18th. During that evening, I received ministry for an arthritic condition in my right hand, something which I had suffered with for at least three years. Exactly nine days later I became totally free of the pain, I cannot praise and love our Lord enough.

Someone else wrote:

I had a long talk with one of your counsellors regarding healing after forty-six years of rheumatoid arthritis. The following day I went to hospital to get the fluid drained from my knees, and the next morning when I awoke I felt absolutely at peace throughout my whole body. My joints are much more comfortable. I'm walking up and down the stairs normally, my arm is beginning to move again and I feel a new person absolutely.

J hadn't wanted to come for ministry. Audrey had prayed with her the previous year for the arthritis in her hands and she had been healed instantaneously. She admitted when we saw her recently that she had never expected the healing to last, but it had and she flexed her fingers easily to show that she was quite free from arthritis in her hands. There was arthritis elsewhere in her body, however, 'But I won't bother to ask for prayer for it,' she said. 'Anyhow, I'm getting used to living with it.' And then the truth slipped out. She added, 'Anyhow, I don't feel I deserve more healing.'

We replied that of course she wasn't worthy to be healed! None of us is worthy of the love of Jesus! The whole point is that He loves us unconditionally, and that despite our complete unworthiness He loves to pour out His healing upon us. At that she agreed to let us pray with her.

J is about fifty and she had grown up with a marked inferiority complex. Her mother had been a woman of great beauty, and she had always been disparaging about J her daughter, who had been a plain child. J had always felt the pain of rejection, and her problem was that she couldn't believe in her heart that Jesus really loved her. She had eventually married in her forties, but the pain of rejection still ran very deep.

We prayed that the Lord might heal the rejection that had been hurting her all her life, that He might set her completely free so that she might know the wonder of his love for her, and that in doing so He might heal the remainder of her arthritis.

We never actually heard whether the arthritis had been healed, but certainly the Lord ministered to the emotional hurt within her. 'Which of you held my hand while you were praying for me?' she asked. My eyes had been open all the time, and I knew that neither of us had had either of our hands within a foot of her right hand. 'But I distinctly felt somebody holding my hand,' she insisted. There was no other explanation—it must have been the Lord. She went away full of thanks in her heart.

The same thing happened on three other occasions this

139

year and each time with a woman who has been deeply hurt emotionally and has suffered greatly from rejection. Once it was the touch of a hand on the person's right arm, once the touch of a hand on the left arm, and once the woman we were praying for felt someone hold her left hand. Each time, however, my eyes were open all the time we were praying and there was absolutely no human contact.

One of the first people I prayed for when we came to the Healing Mission was a man with multiple sclerosis. He couldn't stand without his stick. I prayed for him and I certainly thought that the Lord had healed him, and I believe he thought so too. In fact there appeared to be no healing and the only other news we had of him was a week or two later when he telephoned asking for the number of another man with a healing ministry.

My confidence in praying for people with multiple sclerosis was badly shaken on that occasion, and for a while I dreaded it when somebody came to me seeking prayer for this complaint. However, the occasion came when we were ministering in Bournemouth and a lady suffering from multiple sclerosis was helped into the room by two people, one on either side of her. I remember she had to be held up whilst Audrey and I prayed for her. It seemed as though the Holy Spirit was touching her powerfully, but after prayer her friends lowered her into her chair again, whilst Audrey and I then separated, each going to different parts of the room to pray for other people.

I remember being mildly disturbed whilst I was praying for someone else when there was an outburst of cheering and clapping and when I had finished praying with that person I asked what the noise had been about. I was told that the lady with MS had walked out of the room. Subsequently, two of her friends wrote to us. They said she had been asked in for coffee by the lady who brought her,

After coffee she was so full of joy and praising the Lord, she got up from the settee and walked across the room. She was able to get down three steps to go home and also bend to put her shoe on that had come off. At a meeting on Thursday evening she was walking and praising the Lord. She seems to be getting stronger each day.

140

We haven't seen anyone healed instantaneously from MS but P too recently told us that after her second time of ministry there was further healing; she had now stopped using her walking stick in her home. We have never seen a person healed of total blindness, but we have seen several people with defective eyesight which has gradually improved after prayer. We have seen deafness healed. B said that he was, 'overwhelmed by the goodness of the Lord' as he had been completely healed of deafness in the left ear. He told us that the specialist had said, 'Well, miracles do happen!' Later, his wife wrote to us, 'It is such a joy to have B, my husband, healed of deafness, joining in things instead of having to stand apart, very largely ignored, as so many deaf people are. Praise the Lord!'

We have seen people healed of addiction of various kinds. The first I knew about C was when her doctor telephoned me on the Monday morning after Audrey and I had got back from our Summer holiday. He told me that she had come to the Healing Service the previous Thursday, one of the team at the Mission had prayed for her and she had been completely healed from addiction to heroin. He said she had rung him up saying that she simply couldn't understand how it was that the desire for heroin was no longer there.

Later she came to see Audrey and me. We never really learned what had led her to that Healing Service in the first place as she certainly hadn't been a Christian then. We talked to her about the Lord, and then as so often seems right, we said to her, 'Why don't you pray a prayer which goes something like this?'

God, I don't know who you are, but I'm prepared to take a chance on you and give myself to you. Will you please reveal yourself to me?

We then stood up with C to pray for her. She felt that gentle push on her chest which so often comes from the Holy Spirit, and she fell backwards under His power. As she got up she said, 'I reckon that was His answer.'

We are always aware that, in encouraging someone to pray

141

a prayer like that, we are literally letting the situation go, so that it is no longer in any way under our control! We encourage the person to look for some reaction from the Lord and rely on Him to provide that reaction!

B's addiction was to alcohol. He came to one of our Thursday evening services scarlet in the face, and told us that he was due to go and be dried out. We prayed with him for a few minutes, and he was completely healed. He never got to being dried out because it wasn't needed, and what amazed his doctor was his blood pressure. It was normal for the first time in several years. We have known B for quite a long time since this happened.

Various people come to us who want to get free from the habit of smoking. We remember a lady coming some years ago with this problem and we said the real way to get free from smoking is simply to seek more and more of Jesus. 'Seek Him with your whole heart and you will find that He takes away the desire to smoke.' She came to see us a couple of months later and she told us that this was precisely what had happened, 'I felt I had simply got to have a cigarette,' she said, 'and I went round to the tobacconist before breakfast and came back with three packets of cigarettes. But as I stood in my kitchen, I just looked at them and I said to myself, "These are horrid things." ' She threw them straight into the bin, and had no desire to smoke again from that moment onwards.

A man came up to me after the evening service at the Mission for ministry, saying that his problem, too, was smoking and that he wanted to be free. I explained to him that the best way to become free was to seek more and more of Jesus; but I said that naturally I would be only too happy to pray for the power of the Holy Spirit to fall upon him. Not for the first time, the Lord proved me wrong, as He healed him then and there from the desire to smoke.

B is a lady who often comes to our healing services. She must be in her early seventies; she is small in stature, but great in faith. We had been praying for her mouth for some while. She was due to have major surgery on it and for several

142

weeks before she went into hospital she had been unable to take the wafers at our Communion services unless they had first been dipped into the wine and thus softened. She went into hospital for her surgery on a Wednesday and she robustly told all the nurses that God had healed her. They didn't take her seriously and she submitted to being prepared for an operation on the Thursday morning. She was allowed no breakfast, just a cup of tea. Then about mid-morning she was taken down to see the specialist.

He examined her mouth closely. Then he looked in amazement and said, 'You've had a spontaneous healing'. B rounded on him, 'That's not true,' she said, 'God has healed me'. The specialist smiled and told her that there was no point in her waiting any longer in the hospital; she could go home.

But sometimes the Lord just looks to the faith of the person who is ministering. Usually when someone comes in, we look first at their relationship with the Lord. With F, however, it just didn't seem that that was possible. F was an Irish bachelor in his early seventies who, towards the end of his working life, had been a porter in a large office block in London. He had had a rather narrow religious training and we sensed that it would have been no good to have talked to him about Jesus. We therefore stood up and we prayed.

F's problem was in his left foot. He had only been able to get into the Mission with the help of a walking frame. After we had prayed for him, he sat down again in the chair and as we talked I noticed that he was rubbing his left leg. 'Funny,' he said, 'I can feel a sort of warmth going up and down my leg'.

F was healed. Just to make sure we took him to the foot of the stairs, whilst I held his walking frame, and we suggested that he walked up the stairs. He climbed quickly to the top of the stairs and then came down equally easily. There was no doubt that he had been healed. Indeed, when Audrey rang the doorbell a quarter of an hour later, it was F who opened the door for her, and this time he was carrying his walking frame.

Although it hadn't seemed right to lead F to the Lord

before praying for him, there was no question but that F left the Mission with great joy and full of praises to Jesus.

There was another time when a physical healing led to the person becoming a Christian. M wrote to us:

You have been praying for my brother D. He was in hospital with a very bad heart, hardened arteries, something wrong with his blood, thrombosis in both legs and swollen with water. We were told that he would never leave hospital alive, he was so desperately ill. But I want to thank you for all your prayers, but above all else I want to say, "Thank you, Lord". Oh bless Him, He is a wonderful God, and it amazes me continually to think that He is my very own Heavenly Father. I am so exuberant because D is not only home, he is walking out two long walks a day and breathing normally; looks healthy and happy and the last check-up proved that his arteries are fine. He is now a Christian and reading the Bible, and he talks of these things without any shyness now. Needless to say, the Lord has lifted a great burden from me, bless Him.

# 14

# Love that Heals—2

We don't often see two miracles in a day, but we did, recently. That was an exciting day! When A first came to see Audrey and me, she had only been able to get here with two people to accompany her. The second time she came she had managed with one person; the day she came for the third time, she came alone from South London. Her trouble was paranoia, and on this third occasion, she told us that she'd had no trace of paranoia since her first visit to us.

This was an occasion of great rejoicing for us, because A, who was about forty, had had a long history of mental illness; she had been a patient at Rampton, and, as a punishment, was once put in a padded cell,—where, incidentally, she had come to know the Lord! She told us that she had had no mattress, no clothing, not even sanitation. She just knelt and prayed to the Lord asking Him to keep her *sane.* 'I immediately felt a real sense that someone was there with me,' she wrote, adding: 'When I came out of that cell I was no longer violent and became very gentle—it was such a surprise to me!'

We were, therefore, thrilled at her healing from paranoia. However, after lunch when the person I was due to see walked into my room, I thought, 'Lord, you have given us one exciting time today; I do understand if this next one is going to be less exciting.' The lady who walked in was about fifty, and she didn't look very receptive to prayer. Indeed, as we started talking, she released a flood of bitterness against her husband.

When she stopped, I tried to explain to her that bitterness and resentment simply block the Lord's healing power so that He cannot work in us. To my surprise and joy, she seemed to understand this at once, and a sincere prayer of repentance followed. We stood up to pray and the Holy Spirit fell powerfully on her. She told me that four years earlier she had fallen out of a third floor window and her hands, which had taken the brunt of the fall, had been damaged. 'But', she said, 'they are definitely better since you prayed.'

That seemed the moment when I really had to step out in faith. I took both her hands in mine, and I prayed to the Lord that He would heal both her hands totally. In a way I was unwise, because I was by then sitting down again, and I should have foreseen that under the power of the Holy Spirit she might collapse again on the floor: which is exactly what she did. But she was small and I was able to catch her so that she didn't hurt herself.

After a few minutes, she was sitting up on the floor, having kicked off her shoes, and was wiggling her toes. She explained that the previous week she had been to an osteopath who had told her that her right leg was half an inch shorter than her left. She asked me if I could see the difference; it was quite clear that, whatever had been the case, both legs were now exactly the same length. I said, 'I don't actually believe that the Lord has grown your leg by half an inch while we have been praying. I think what is much more likely is that your pelvis was knocked out of alignment when you fell out of that window; that could easily give the impression of one leg being longer than the other. I think what happened,' I said, 'was that the imbalance in the pelvis was healed when I prayed that last time, and that the pelvis coming back into its natural position, the legs were then the same length again.'

'I believe that's so,' she said. 'As you were talking about the pelvis coming back into position, I could feel the warmth of His healing power in the pelvic region.'

Sometimes people come to us with marriage problems. In July last year we ministered to a young wife who was at the end of her tether. She was married to a young man who had been in prison in Broadmoor for ten years and communication

146

between them had completely broken down. He had been so deeply hurt emotionally that he just couldn't open up and talk. He did, however, come to see me subsequently and we talked and prayed together. Then in November he telephoned and I jotted down his words.

He exclaimed, 'Prayer proved to be the answer; we are now expecting our first baby! Thank you, and thank the Lord so much.'

B's marriage situation was one we had prayed for, for some time, when she telephoned last summer. Her husband had been living with another woman for two and a half years, but she now telephoned to say that he was coming back to her and to thank us for our prayers. Recently we heard from T and K, praising God that, after prayer, they had come back together again. K had become a Christian, had cancelled the divorce and both were living together again in their old home with their children.

P was married to a successful architect but the marriage had broken down. She said her husband never appreciated anything she did and he treated her like a doormat. Consequently she had moved out and she had spent the last few months living in the garden house. She had had a sad life; she was fostered and had suffered a great deal of rejection with her parents not wanting her, and once she had tried to commit suicide.

We led her to Jesus and she made a real confession of all that was wrong in her life. We then asked Jesus to give her a deep love for her husband and to ease the way for her going back to live at home again. We asked Him, too, to open her husband's heart to her needs and to bring them together in a real relationship of love. As we prayed, the power of the Spirit fell on her, and she fell to the ground and received the gift of tongues. Now she is back with her husband. 'He is being so kind to me,' she says, and she tells us she is so overwhelmed with God's love for her that she feels that she can't stop praying in tongues! They have two children, and are a happy and united family.

Sometimes people have been so emotionally damaged that they are not able to sustain a stable relationship. J came to see us one day. She was an attractive woman of thirty-six but as soon as someone began to come close to her she got worried and broke off the relationship. She had had many childhood hurts, but her main difficulty, as with so many people, was accepting the love of Jesus, and trusting Him. She felt so worthless and she was sure she would never make anyone happy. We went straight into prayer with her, and the Lord in His graciousness showed her what she meant to Him and how He loved her. She came twice for ministry and after the second time she was able to form a lasting relationship which has since led to marriage. Six months later a woman came up to Audrey in a church where we were ministering and thanked her for our help to J. J, she said, was now very happily married.

It is not only the relationship between man and wife that so often needs healing. One day, a lady of about fifty-five came to see us at the Mission. She was a widow, and had one son, now in his thirties, whom she had always adored. Having lost her husband she had no one close to her but her son. However, when her son married, he had turned against his mother through the influence of his wife. He had two children aged seven and five but his mother had never seen her grandchildren. She used to telephone him in the City, where he worked, but he always refused to speak to her. This broke her heart, as, until his marriage, they had always been so close. 'What can I do?' she said. We told her she must hand everything over to Jesus. 'He loves your son more than even you do', we said, 'He will sort this out if you will only let Him.' We spent a long time in prayer, and she came to the point where she could forgive her son and her daughter-in-law, and lift the whole burden to her Heavenly Father, trusting Him to work a miracle in this situation.

About a fortnight later, she telephoned. She was so over-come with emotion that she could hardly get the words out. She had telephoned her son and he had been like he always used to be. She realised that the Lord had started to heal the relationship, 'Oh,' she exclaimed, 'God is just so wonderful!'

M, a widow in her fifties, told us that her mother, aged

eighty-eight, whom she dearly loved, for some reason, the previous year, had turned against her, and now didn't want to speak to her, and was cruel and bitter. When she wrote to her mother the letters were torn up, unread. She said she had no idea of the reason, and was very, very hurt and in tears about it. She had asked her sisters what was wrong, but they had no idea.

We prayed with her, and the Lord seemed to say that she should write a letter to her mother, praying very much before she wrote it, and asking the Lord to guide her pen by His spirit, so that she should write the right words. It then seemed that she should send this letter to her sister, asking her to read it to her mother.

The sister received this letter, took it to her mother and read it. The mother could not believe she had written it. She was so touched by this letter, that the barrier was broken, and the family are now re-united. M said, now with tears of joy in her eyes: 'I am overwhelmed at the goodness of the Lord, and how He guides us when we ask Him.'

It is so rewarding for us who work at the Mission when we see human relationships healed like this. In the same way it is rewarding when a physical healing and a spiritual release come together. We have had lovely letters testifying to this. Recently this letter arrived in the post:

I had (inner) healing, and was greatly excited later to find that I had a physical healing of my knee as well, which I hadn't realised at the time. A friend remarked later, "The swelling has gone and your knee has changed shape!"

At the same time I certainly received the Baptism of the Holy Spirit which has remained quietly bubbling, and not so quiet at times! And I don't think I have ever felt so happily well. Now about the gift of tongues. Not knowing very much about it I have just used it every day in praise and intercession and just giving over to let the Holy Spirit say what He wanted to! How difficult to express in writing!

I have been amazed how every day things have happened and I have felt challenged: "Why don't you ask for greater things?"

Often it is impossible to put into words just what happens when somebody is healed emotionally. As we look back over some of the thanksgivings we have received, they are so brief and one is left to guess at the depth of healing which lies behind them. A friend wrote last summer, 'My mind is free now for the first time in ten years.' M wrote a few months earlier, 'I'm definitely feeling better in myself, after ministry at the Mission,' adding, 'Jesus is nearer to me, and somehow life is not just the empty muddle it was before.' Another wrote later giving thanks for a vision the Lord gave her during ministry here. She saw a heavy cloak of fear being lifted from her, and herself walking away from it as it fell off. 'It was just such a release,' she said, and she has not been troubled by fear since.

Sometimes, however, people write much more fully. T wrote to us:

Some years ago I came to the Mission for counsel, and received much healing in the way of deliverance and a broken heart. But my diabetic illness remained, no matter how I tried to exercise faith. Now I feel God Himself has given me the answer. Take God's medicine (His Word) as often you would a prescribed pill, and expect it to heal you. Proverbs 4 verses 20-22 was how I started off on this voyage of discovery, *"My son, pay attention to what I say, listen closely to my words. Do not let them out of your sight, keep them within your heart. For they are life to those that find them and health to a man's whole body."*

This week I was told by my doctor after lots of tests, etc., that I now have angina. I went home to think about this, and I realised that doctors could do much to help me, but they could not *heal*, only God could do that. I spent one afternoon seeking God about this, and that is when I found out about God's medicine and all that it does *if* applied correctly and allowed to work internally in the heart. I have practised hearing the Word for a long time, but I did not realise that God also wanted me to swallow it and digest it as well. How simple when God explains it to you.

I now feel I have my feet on the pathway to real health. Based on what God alone can do for me, I'm expecting a miracle to take place. Man says this disease is incurable. God's Word says that Jesus took *all* our sicknesses, so I'm going to believe that God can do it; wants to do it; has done it and made provision for it. Now I must learn to receive all these provisions and feed from them. I have a sense within me that I will be writing soon to say that God has done the miracle for me.

It was in fact less than three weeks later that T wrote again:

On Monday evening this week, the Lord was teaching me about how safe I was in Jesus, that nothing would happen to me that wouldn't be used for my good, and the tremendous truth that Satan did not have power over my life now because Jesus had it. *"Greater is He that is in you than he that is in the world."* I meditated on this all evening.

The next morning I awoke feeling a little under the weather. I steadily got worse. A heart attack came on, and I knew I was going to black out under the pain. But in my spirit I called out to Jesus and confessed to Him my weakness and how vulnerable I was feeling and please would He come to my aid. Jesus came to me and said, "Speak to him", meaning Satan. So I did. I told him that I refused to accept this heart attack and I quoted scripture after scripture as the Holy Spirit brought them to my mind. It seemed like ages, but in time it was only about two minutes. Then miraculously the pain vanished, the pounding in my ears disappeared and the hissing noise stopped.

I knew without a shadow of a doubt that Satan had tried to kill me, and Jesus had allowed that attack in order to prove to me whom to trust. I now know that Jesus will always come to my aid and that I have *no* strength: *He is my strength.* I knew it was common sense to be resting, but I jumped out of bed, took a shower, had a large breakfast and continued my day rejoicing. My husband was amazed when I told him about this and together we gave thanks. Since then I have had a chance to share this with other Christians for God to receive the glory.

Now I am much stronger in my faith as I intercede for others. I know God has no favourites, and will do for them just the same wonderful things that He has done for me. I am continuing to be taught every day more and more of God's ways and I find it so fascinating that it is all so simple. We make everything so complicated, don't we?

We are always interested at the way the Lord seems to love

working through people who are complete beginners. Perhaps this is because they have no human confidence and they just have to depend on Him. The other day J came to join the team here at the Mission. We think her coming here had been quite an act of faith. After all, when people work here, they are expected to pray for sick people, and they are expected to expect results! It can be quite challenging. J was thrilled because the very first day someone rang, asking for prayer on the telephone, it was a lady with an ulcer in her eye; J prayed; and half an hour later the lady telephoned again to say that the ulcer was already going. What an encouragement!

But so many people find that the Lord can use them even in small things. A friend wrote to us from Reading,

> I thought you might be interested in how God is developing a little "Healing Ministry" through me quite wonderfully. As I am now at home all day, home is my base. I work with the Chaplain at the University, counselling/befriending the students and all sorts of good things are going on there. Also, all sorts of people of all ages either "pop in" for a coffee or a meal or else I go along to visit them for some quite innocuous reason, and every time, in ways big and small, God uses the opportunity, sometimes for healing, sometimes for teaching, sometimes just to talk about Christ. It is quite lovely but totally unstructured and led by Him. No two days are the same, and the range of people and problems encountered is widening and deepening. It is all terribly informal and low-key and right for the surroundings. Being a female, hugging people and holding their hands while praying with them, or simply touching them lightly with a silent prayer inside is a natural thing to do, and where people are shy of healing, prayer can be a real help to breaking down barriers. I have never been so happy or fulfilled in all my life.

People may telephone us for prayer for big things or for little things. C wrote to tell us that after prayer on the telephone she had her lump removed—and it was benign. She wrote, 'I can't express how thankful I am. I am also much freer of pain in my back for which I also asked for prayer.'

With L, however, it was just 'flu, tiresome as that can be. His mother rang in to say that after prayer over the telephone, his 'flu left completely and he was able to go to school the following day.

We are always deeply grateful to the six hundred or more people who pray for us every day—our intercessors, as we call them. One of them wrote recently,

One of the things God has been impressing on me lately is that I did not become an intercessor of my own choice but that *He chose me*. This has relieved me of all feelings of inadequacy and inferiority for I know that God will use me as a channel. He puts the desire to pray within me; I then pray as directed by Him, and the rest is His responsibility. I just sit back and watch Him go to work on the problems, solving them in mind-boggling ways that leave me breathless with astonishment, or thrilled by His incredible patience. God seems to be saying that He wants His intercessors to be like watchmen who call His attention to every situation; our job stops there as God then moves in. He may want to use us as answers, and if we are alert we will hear Him telling us what to do, where to go and how to behave. Obedience is our *key* to becoming prayer warriors. I praise and thank God that He is equipping His army by teaching us all about prayer warfare.

Our intercessors come from every walk of life. Recently we had this lovely letter from R, who is in prison in Scotland:

It will always be part of my testimony that as a prisoner of man, I can look out over the wall and see prisoners of Satan. But I know that because of a very sinless, brave and wonderful man, giving His life for me, I am *free*! Thanks be to the Lord. I only hope that the people I see outside this prison, and indeed inside it, will quickly ask the Lord Jesus for parole so they, too, can be free. Therefore, once again I thank you all for your care and love and I enclose your form and am pleased to become a servant of the Lord Jesus.

We have welcomed R as yet another of the intercessors who pray so faithfully for our work here.

Perhaps S represented one of the more dramatic cases of

the Lord using someone who was a complete beginner. She came to us one evening some six months ago. She is thirty-two, unmarried, and a successful business woman. She had, however, been off work, mentally ill, for three months. Her problem was nightmares, and they were particularly tormenting. She had been in a well-known mental hospital in London, but had discharged herself after a week because she had realised that her problem was not in fact mental but spiritual. Practically each day, however, since she left the hospital they had telephoned her or her brother saying, 'She must come back; her only hope of regaining sanity is to come back.'

Things had got so bad that a few nights before she came to see us, S had kept herself awake all night, simply because she couldn't bear a recurrence of the nightmares. The following night she had slept from sheer exhaustion, and the nightmares had again been appalling. We felt that unless something happened, it could only be a few days before she committed suicide. She thought so too.

It was one of those lovely situations where the Lord had obviously been working quietly in S's heart before He brought her to us. It was so easy for us to lead her to Jesus, to lead her to repent of her sins and to accept His forgiveness and His love, and His healing.

She was already looking very different from when she came in. Then she started to tell us about her flat. There was something horrid about her bedroom in the flat she had moved into not many months before, she told us. We told her that as a Christian, she could take the authority of Jesus and dismiss any unclean presence that might be in her bedroom.

S told us later that when she returned to her flat she tried to enter her room and had literally been blown backwards out of her room by, as it were, a noiseless explosion. She then had the presence of mind to follow the advice that we had given her. She took an ordinary bowl from the kitchen drawer, put some water in it, put her hand over the water, and said, 'I bless this water in the name of God, the Father, the Son, Jesus, and the Holy Spirit, Amen.' She then went back into her room and she commanded, in the Name of Jesus, that any unclean presence in that room should leave, never to return. She then dipped her fingers in the water and lightly sprinkled her room with the water.

The next time she came to see us she told us that she then went to bed and slept soundly right through the night. She has never again been troubled by nightmares.

We had occasion to put this to the test again when we were asked to go to a house in Fulham. It was a perfectly ordinary house in a long row of terraced houses, and there were three girls in their late teens living there. It was the mother of one of them who asked us to help. It sounded as though there were poltergeists in the house. It hadn't worried them very much, that furniture was moved about during the night. Quite often, apparently, they would go to bed with the hi-fi equipment on the table, and come down in the morning to find it on the floor, or the other way round. What did frighten them, though, was when one of the girls had been sitting at the end of the long sitting room which went from front to back of the house, smoking a cigarette, and the telephone had rung at the other end of the room. She put her cigarette down on the ashtray next to her, walked over to answer the telephone, and her lighted cigarette came and joined her, settling in her lap. In addition there were various other manifestations of poltergeist activity.

The house was on the edge of a cemetery, and we wondered if it was haunted, for in the old days a person who had committed suicide was buried outside a cemetery. When Audrey and I went to the house, we started with a short, informal Communion Service, asking the Lord to give peace to any restless spirit that might be causing the trouble. We then did exactly as we had told S to do. We blessed some water from the kitchen and we went into each room of the house, one by one, commanding any unclean spirit or any poltergeist to leave and to go to Jesus, never to return. We did this with each room, with the hall, the stairs, the landing and indeed, the garden.

We were therefore rather concerned when, a week later, the

mother of one of the girls telephoned and said that the previous night there had been a lot of trouble again. They had been kept awake all night by footsteps walking up and down in the roof and a lot of banging. We realised that the one part of the house we had not been to was the attic!

We returned to the house, and with a certain amount of trepidation, Audrey and I climbed up the ladder and through the trap door into the attic. The roof was low, the maximum height must have been about four feet, and there were no floor boards. Also, there was no communicating door or opening with the next door house on either side. It was clear that the footsteps and the banging had again been from the poltergeists. This time we took care that every corner of the attic was covered as we commanded any unclean thing to leave in the name of Jesus and never to return, and we sprinkled it all with water which we had blessed. They never again had any trouble in that house.

Quite often people come to us for this sort of ministry, and in some ways we see it as one of the easier forms of ministry. All that is needed is to be certain in one's heart that Jesus really is Lord; that when He shed His blood on the cross He broke the power of Satan, once and for all, and that, provided one perseveres, one simply cannot help winning in His Name. Harm is, however, being done nowadays by 'amateur exorcists', and we think it is usually better to keep off the subject. It is, however, worth adding that of the people who come to us saying firmly, 'I need deliverance', probably half of them don't need anything of the sort! So often, it is simply a case of a person suffering the temptation and oppression from Satan which always seeks to spoil the Christian life at one time or another.

The practice of having a Communion service for a restless spirit, perhaps someone who has not received a Christian burial, is one which, like so much to do with the Christian faith, I find a mystery. I know at least one man with a tremendous ministry of teaching, who says that Christians should not pray for the dead. At the same time, I know of another Christian who frequently has Communion services for a relative who might have died without a Christian burial, and sometimes a healing follows.

For our part, where a woman has either had an abortion or a miscarriage, we do find that there is often great comfort if we have a simple Communion for the little being that never reached the point of normal birth, and the mother names it.

N, who is now nearly eighty, came to see us. Many years ago she had had a miscarriage; she had also had an abortion, 'Do you believe in life after death?' we asked. 'Of course,' she replied. We agreed, therefore, that the two unborn babies must be living on, somewhere. 'What are their names?' we asked. 'I'd never thought of naming them,' came the reply. She prayed, asking the Lord. A few moments later, she said it was quite clear that they were both boys, and without hesitation she told us their names.

A few days later she wrote to us, 'After leaving you and walking out of the Mission the most glorious thing happened. As I looked up into the most beautiful starlit night I saw a big star, and behind the star, the Lord standing with each arm round a young man, and I knew what that meant. It was Jesus with my two sons showing me the blessing of confession and His forgiveness. I just stood watching that vision in the street, and after a while I walked to the bus stop and could still see the vision and the star as I looked up.'

How much there is which we don't understand about the Christian faith! But if we understood it all, we would ourselves be God.

We close this chapter by coming back to an essentially practical situation. L is in his thirties; he is in full-time Christian work, and when he came to see us he was in a real financial jam. He and his wife had felt that it was right for them to befriend a man from their church. He was a lawyer, and they had given him a signature on their bank account and, to put it bluntly, they had been conned. He had gone through all their money and had left them heavily in debt. In addition and at the same time, L's job had gone wrong. They were having to sell their small home to pay off the debts, and so L found himself with a wife and three small children, the youngest only thirteen weeks old, with no home and no job. Small wonder that he was desperate.

Immediately our hearts bled for any man who could find himself in such a grave situation. We then realised that we must not lose faith in the Lord. 'The Lord has allowed this to happen, L,' we said. 'We believe that he has allowed all this precisely to test your faith. You must be robust about this and thank Him for what has happened. In His love for you, He has knocked away the human props on which we all rely in this world, precisely so that you can depend entirely on Him. Trust Him and all will come right.'

It was strong stuff, but underneath L was a mature Christian. He accepted it. He asked the Lord to forgive him for his lack of faith, and already one could see the peace of God coming on him once again. We prayed and as we were praying at twenty-five past six that night, we found ourselves praying for L's wife. The poor girl must be distraught with worry at home, not knowing what would happen. We found ourselves praying that the Lord would help her, not just sometime that evening, but that He would help her precisely at that moment when we were praying. It was certainly an act of faith on our part to pray like that.

About a quarter of an hour later, when we had finished praying and when L was obviously so much happier, I said 'Do telephone your wife from here and tell her that you feel happier.' I left him in the room to talk to her privately. I went upstairs to my room on the ground floor, and a few moments later I heard him coming up the stairs two at a time. He burst into my room. 'Good News!' he shouted. I asked him what had happened. 'At twenty-five past six, precisely the time you prayed, somebody telephoned my wife and offered her financial help.' He said.

Who says that God doesn't answer prayer!

# Delivered to your door...

Or to a friend's! Get yourself a free catalog subscription, or sign up a pal who seeks good deals on great clothes. Just mail in the card, call 1-800-356-4444, fax us at 1-800-332-0103 or visit us at landsend.com, providing the information below.

NAME

E-MAIL

(We'll send our e-newsletter with great specials and stories!)

ADDRESS

CITY

STATE                                    ZIP

PHONE (        )

1.800.356.4444 or landsend.com
*Please mention Dept. LE-69*

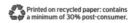

## 15

# And if They are not Healed?

Often the explanation for seemingly unanswered prayer is that we have simply prayed with the wrong emphasis. We, being human, have merely prayed for the healing of the physical ailment. The Lord has wanted to perform a deeper healing as when He healed that Indian lady's resentment. If we had simply prayed for healing of the lump under her tongue I do not believe it would have been healed. We might then have been tempted to conclude: God didn't want to heal her. Often there may be a deep work to do in a person before the moment has come, in His perfect timing, for the physical healing to take place.

Indeed, there are times when it does not take place. Two or three years ago, my sister Betsy, who was far from well, asked me to anoint her with oil and pray for her healing. We had a lovely time of prayer, sitting in our bedroom. As I prayed, the Lord seemed to be giving me a picture of her, once again as a child but bursting with health and vigour, filled with joy and laughter. I was pretty certain I knew what the Lord was telling me, and sure enough, some two months later, Betsy died. Much as I loved her, and indeed I still miss her a lot, I simply couldn't bring myself to grieve at her funeral. I was just so filled with the knowledge that she was now free of that defective body of hers, that she was united with Jesus for all eternity, and that she was restored to perfect wholeness and healing. Her funeral was a time of great rejoicing, for her sake.

Then there is Joni, the American girl, attractive and

athletic, who at the age of seventeen broke her neck when diving into the sea; she was paralysed from the neck downwards. Her book recounts the struggles she went through, trying to come to terms with this appalling disability. It tells of the countless people who were praying for her physical healing. But Joni has not been healed physically. Indeed in her book she says she had now reached the point where she can genuinely give thanks to the Lord that she hasn't been healed. If she had been healed, she writes, she would merely be one of millions of American suburban housewives and mothers, whereas, as it is, the Lord has given her a ministry to thousands of people, both within America and overseas. I believe that the many prayers which were offered up to the Lord for her physical healing were indeed used by Him to release His power, but in her case to refine her spiritually, so that He was then able to use her more powerfully than if He had simply released His power to heal her body. Sometimes, when the Lord doesn't heal physically, it is because He wants to do something even more wonderful for us.

Of course in the area of healing, much depends on what one might call the 'expectancy level'. We read that in His own home town, Nazareth, even Jesus was only able to heal a few people.[59] The expectancy level there was very low; they simply did not expect to see people healed—and only a few of them were. I think faith, indeed, is rather like a motor car. A motor car normally goes forwards, but it is possible to make it go backwards. Faith is praying with the expectancy that something will happen. But if one is convinced that it is not going to happen, faith works in reverse. I believe one can positively impede the working of our Lord's will, by doubts and negative thoughts, believing in one's heart that nothing is going to happen. We remember Job's words: 'What I feared has come upon me.'[60]

The uncle of a friend of mine conducted a healing mission is South Africa, between the wars. He came back saying that the proportion of healings among the black population was higher than among the white. The white people in South

Africa had the benefit of being educated, the black people by contrast were uneducated and simple; they just found it easier to accept that Jesus, in His love, longed to heal them.

Again, we remember the story we were told by Reg and Lucia East, who began the ministry at Whatcombe House in Dorset. A neighbouring farmer had a herd of dairy cows, and they all contracted some bovine disease. As a result, the farmer was daily expecting an order from the Ministry of Agriculture to have the whole herd destroyed. They rang up Reg and Lucia, who happily went round with stools and sat among the straw and manure in the farmyard. They prayed for the healing of those cows, and all indeed were healed. Now, no one is going to claim that those cows had some deep spiritual and bovine faith, but it does seem self-evident that 'faith in reverse' was not in evidence on that occasion. Clearly, the cows were neutral in regard to faith. They had no in-built education and training, pressurising their minds to believe that prayer was without power and nothing would happen. As we pray, in line with His will, it is so important for us to remember Jesus' words, 'Whatever you ask for in prayer, believe that you have received it and it will be yours.'[61]

However, as we pray for someone's healing, it is vital to be following where the Holy Spirit leads us, and not as it were, to get ahead of God. I remember the Rev. John Barr, speaking to the Lloyd's Christian Union in the City of London, telling a terrible story of how he had seen a group of people praying for a lady in a wheelchair. They prayed for her healing; they then urged her to claim her healing and to stand up in faith. I remember John saying that one of the most terrible sounds he has ever heard was as the lady tried to get to her feet, and he actually heard her bones breaking under the unaccustomed weight. Never in any way, must we attempt to manipulate God. It is for us to follow where He leads.

The Lord doesn't reserve the gifts of healing for special people. I don't believe that healing is a prerogative of the clergy. Anyone in a church or fellowship ought to be open to the thought that the Lord may want to use them for healing. It is important, also, to be ready to minister the healing love of Jesus within one's own family.

There is healing through the service of Holy Communion. Two of the earliest occasions when I prayed for somebody to be healed of cancer, were immediately after I had taken the eight o'clock Holy Communion service. In one case a person I was talking to, as people left the church, said that he had got cancer. In the other case, a lady told me that her brother had got cancer. In each case I merely asked the half dozen people who were nearest, to gather round, and in the space of perhaps half a minute, each of us with our hands on the next person's shoulders, standing in a circle, we just prayed that the Lord would heal the person involved of cancer. In each case the prayer was answered.

A problem which often arises, is the difficulty of keeping one's healing. Quite often it happens that someone is healed, but the healing seems to be temporary, and then the sickness, whether it be physical, or indeed mental, comes back to them. One of the ways of keeping one's healing, is to keep thanking the Lord that one has been healed. Not many weeks ago, I went to bed with a temperature after lunch, knowing that I had got a bout of 'flu. I got up the following morning because M was coming to see me at a quarter to ten, and I didn't want to let her down. But I still had a temperature. As it happened, I finished ministering to her a quarter of an hour early, and I said, 'Now it's your turn.' She asked what I meant. I said that I had got 'flu, I still had a temperature, and I wanted her to pray for me to be healed.

I think M was rather taken aback. 'How can I pray for you, a clergyman?' she said. 'And anyhow,' she added, 'I wouldn't know what to say.' I told her that I wasn't in the least interested in the difficulties. She was a Christian, and would she please get on and pray for me; I wanted to be healed. I then found myself on the receiving end of five minutes of lovely prayer, clearly inspired by the Holy Spirit. At the end of this, I felt completely different, and indeed, M said to me that before she had prayed, my face had looked ashen, and

162

she knew I ought to be in bed. But she said that, as she was praying, she actually saw the colour coming back into my cheeks.

On several occasions during that day, I was aware of the voice of Satan, trying to steal my healing from me. I had to be quite firm and resolute with him and tell him that I was listening to no such lies. Jesus had healed me and that was that. I kept on praising Jesus for healing me. Such being the case, there was no relapse. I worked a perfectly normal day until we went to bed eventually at about eleven o'clock that night.

Early this year, a couple in their fifties or sixties came down from Derbyshire for ministry. He had a malignant tumour on his lung—which was healed over the following three months—and she suffered from acute sciatica. Subsequently, she wrote to me as follows:

> I left the Healing Mission that day completely free from pain, and not even twinges or stiffness for the following twenty-four hours, which is better than I have been for the past five months. But two nights later, after going upstairs, pains came on worse than ever. It took me about thirty-six hours till I got over this shock, and then I sat in the Lord's presence, and asked Him to bring me back into the calm and peace which I had known during your ministering. Praise God, the sense of His peace and presence returned, and also the healing!
>
> This time I have been receiving progressive healing, not all at once. It is as though I learn to receive His healing each time the affliction tries to come back; I keep believing it, and I *know* beyond a shadow of a doubt the nerve pains of sciatica are on the way out, completely and for good! Praise the Lord. I am going upstairs easily, and even if I have stiffness, on awaking in the morning, as I ignore it and walk about, it leaves me.
>
> I think I made a mistake in the past by not bothering to try and get full healing for so many years. It did not seem important to me until I began to be crippled, earlier this year.

A month later, the same lady wrote:

> When I first had that come-back of pain, my disappointment was

so great, I thought all was lost. When I let common sense come in, I realised that I *had* been healed, and therefore it *must* be God's will for me to stay healed. The rest you know. I can truly say today I'm totally healed. Praise His Name. It was quite a battle for a few weeks, but I was convinced (as I always have been) that all sickness is the work of Satan. Every time he had to withdraw the symptoms, I was free longer, and now he hardly ever tries it on—just a short sharp twinge which may assail me once a week, and then I remember that I am healed, and it leaves me.

Sometimes it seems that the Lord wants to heal a person, but that He wants first to use their infirmity to stimulate them into taking a more positive attitude—to make a greater effort to get close to Him, and to draw on His power. My mind goes to a person whom Audrey is ministering to at the present time. Neither doctors nor psychiatrists can help her, and yet her suffering is real. Each time that Audrey prays for her, there is a slight improvement. But by nature she is a negative person, and she is beginning to realise that if this affliction is to be overcome, in the strength of our Lord, she has got to become more positive, and to step out in faith herself, rather than, as comes more naturally to her, sitting back and expecting somebody else's prayers to do the job. I am quite clear that she will not be freed from this affliction until the Lord has used it to stimulate her into living more positively in His strength. When she has done that, two things will follow. Firstly, in the Lord's strength, she will have overcome this suffering in her body, but secondly, she will then be ready to be used by the Lord in a far more powerful ministry than she could be at the present time.

We live, after all, in an age when much of the incentive of earlier centuries has been reduced. Many people go through life without ever exerting themselves physically. For the majority of people, physical hard work has been abolished. The need to make an effort to go here or there, has largely been eliminated by the use of public transport. In the evenings, most people spend several hours watching television, which is a passive entertainment. Whilst there are certainly some good programmes, watching them involves no positive effort. Much of the stimulus which previously was present in life has been removed. I believe as a result many people are negative in their attitude, and the Lord, who longs to perfect his creation in each of us, wants to stimulate us to becoming positive once again.

Many people come to us suffering from depression. This is one of the blights of the present day. The person's thoughts turn inwards to themselves, their wills become flabby, and they give way to self-pity: every depressive who comes to us explains earnestly that no one else can ever understand the particular hell he or she is going through. We try and get them to renounce their depression before God, and to accept that He loves them and indeed is longing to help them get out of the depression. The goal is for them to turn outwards to Him, to be obedient to Him and love Him and to let His healing light flow into them.

Sometimes the causes of depression are partly physical. It is always worth trying a course of pills containing Vitamin B6, sometimes there may be a thyroid deficiency—even a good brisk walk each day can help, breathing deeply and regularly can help. But *ultimately* the depression derives from Satan. How could a God who is perfect love have deliberately created the black despair which weighs on the depressive?

In the book of Job, in the Old Testament, we read that the Lord allowed Satan to afflict Job. The same is true today. Most Christians experience Satan attacking them in one way or another. I believe the Lord allows this in order to stimulate us so that we may draw on His strength at a deeper level than we have been able to hitherto. He allows Satan to afflict us, precisely so that we can learn to defeat Satan in our lives. I don't believe He ever allows Satan to batter us with the objective of our continuing to be oppressed by him.

Often we are not taught nearly enough about how to identify Satan's voice, and how to deal with him. The first step must be to identify him. The voice of the Lord is that still, small voice of calm and peace, which Elijah heard. Satan, by contrast, tries to speak to us with doubts, with feelings of guilt and unworthiness, and through fear. Jesus indeed described Satan as 'the father of all lies',[62] and as 'the accuser of the brethren'.[63] He often comes disguised as an angel of light.[64]

Feelings of guilt are very real, and I believe they come from Satan. The feeling of guilt does not build up a person, it drags them down—it is in the nature of Satan to drag somebody down. If you think back to an instance in your life when you deliberately sinned, I believe that you longed to be washed clean, to put that particular sin right behind you, and never think of it again, to turn to the Lord and seek His total forgiveness. The Bible calls this 'repentance', and when we repent, the Lord always forgives us, so we know that any further feelings of guilt are from Satan and as such are to be rejected.

As with feelings of guilt, so feelings of worthlessness are also from Satan. It is of course a lie that any of us are worthless. The Lord loves each and every one of us, and if we are of such value in His eyes, it must be a lie when Satan tries to put the thought into our minds that we are worthless.

Sometimes people feel that by sinning in this way or that, they have put themselves beyond the ability of God to forgive them. Sometimes, indeed, people come to us, believing that they have committed the unforgivable sin.[65] I venture to think that the only unforgivable sin is the sin which is not repented of. We have known a person, who for thirty years was deep into the occult, including the worship of Satan and the denigration of God, thus turning right and wrong completely upside down. We have seen her completely set free and forgiven. Provided people come to the Lord humbly and seeking His forgiveness, we have yet to meet anybody who has not received His bountiful forgiveness and love.

Worry and fear are of Satan. As St John wrote 'Perfect love drives out fear',[66] and the love of God is perfect. Satan will also try and put into our minds doubts as to the truth of God's word in the Bible. This is where we need to 'take up the shield of faith',[67] as St Paul wrote, and to stand on the facts as set forth in the Bible.

Having identified the voice of Satan lying to us, we need to rebuke him. I remember David Watson teaching us to speak out along these lines:

> Satan, I've caught you at your tricks again, trying to fill me with doubt/fear/guilt. You know perfectly well that Jesus broke your power when He gave Himself on the cross, for me, on Calvary; and you know perfectly well that I belong to Jesus and that I have given myself to Him. Therefore, Satan, in the name of Jesus My Lord, I command you on His authority to stop pestering me and to go.

The first two steps are to identify Satan and to rebuke him. But there is a third step. We need immediately to turn to the Lord and to praise Him, either in English, or if we have been given the gift of tongues, in tongues. Otherwise Satan, having been dismissed, just turns round and has another go. But having dismissed Satan once, don't let's go on doing it! Instead let's keep on praising Jesus for His victory.

Quite often people come to us saying they gave their lives to the Lord a few years earlier, and they are worried because the first vividness of enthusiasm has gone. They find it difficult to pray, and they are no longer aware of the presence of Jesus. How can they get back the lovely rapture of their early days as Christians? Often the answer lies in repentance, followed by total commitment to the Lord. Furthermore, if we are looking for 'feelings' we won't find them. Often, indeed, the Lord will deliberately withdraw the 'feelings', in order to stimulate us to take our stand upon the word of God in the Bible and increase our faith. When we have stepped out in faith, and made it clear that we are going to press on in our walk with the Lord, trusting in what we know to be true, then in His love and kindness, He will give us back the feelings, when, in His love, He knows that we are ready.

We remember Jesus' words to His followers, 'Be perfect, therefore, as your Heavenly Father is perfect.'[68] We remember, too, the words in Peter's first letter, when he quotes God as saying, 'Be holy, because I am holy.'[69]

There are two ways in which we can take these commands,

that we should be perfect and holy, like God, Himself. We can on the one hand say that Jesus was a young man whose style of speaking was hyperbole, and indeed it is true that at times He exaggerated to make His point. There was the time when He rebuked His followers for trying to pick out a speck of dust in their neighbour's eye, when they had a great beam of wood in their own eye. How could anyone have a great beam, many feet long, in their eye! Clearly He was exaggerating to make His point. We may, therefore, if we wish, take the view that Jesus never really meant us to be perfect, and that all He wanted us to be was good, decent people. If we take that interpretation of what Jesus said, there is really very little reason for any of us to repent. Most of us are pretty decent people anyhow, and we would say that, judged by that standard, we haven't got much to repent of.

But alternatively, you can take at face value Jesus' words, and the words that Peter quotes from the Old Testament. It must be in the will of God to change each of us, to clothe each of us with His own nature and His own likeness, so that eventually we are indeed perfect as He is. If we accept that standard for ourselves, then we just need to fall down before the Lord, and say, 'Lord, I'm going to accept your standard of perfect holiness for me, but Lord, there is nothing in me, of myself, which is perfect or holy.' 'Lord,' we conclude, 'all I can do is to throw myself on your mercy. Wash me clean, Lord, as only you can, and forgive me.'

As we pray thus, we remember Jesus' story of the two men who stood in the synagogue praying.[70] There was the Pharisee who felt he was not like other men. He reminded God that he fasted twice a week, and that he gave away a tenth of his goods to the poor. Then Jesus told about the other man, a tax collector, one of a despised class in those days, who stood at the back of the synagogue, and would not so much as lift his eyes to heaven but beat his breast and said, 'God, have mercy on me a sinner.' Jesus said it was the tax collector who went home justified, rather than the Pharisee.

There are those who argue that we should not hold a view of ourselves which sees us as having in us nothing which, of ourselves, is perfect. But I believe that view is based on an incomplete realisation of the power of forgiveness. It is only as we see ourselves as the Lord in His perfect righteousness and holiness sees us, that we can really cry out from the depths of our heart, asking Him to have mercy on us. It is only as we pray with this deep, deep repentance, that we come to know the freedom and joy of really deep forgiveness. I'm quite sure that shallow repentance is only followed by a shallow awareness of forgiveness. But really deep repentance is followed by the awareness of really deep forgiveness.

Some see repentance as being degrading; they see it as being a self-inflicted process of rubbing one's nose in the mud. I believe this is very far from the truth. I believe that true and deep repentance should be a matter of relief, as we accept ourselves as the Lord sees us, and as there is, in some measure, a meeting of the minds between the Lord and ourselves. As we receive His forgiveness and His freedom, true repentance becomes a matter of joy.

A friend of ours who was a professional psychiatrist, became a Christian, and went into the Church. He has said that if only we could teach repentance and forgiveness to people who are in mental hospitals, half those mental hospitals and psychiatric wards would be emptied overnight. Such, in his view, is the power of repentance and forgiveness.

As we read in the New Testament, 'All have sinned and fallen short of the glory of God.'[71] There is much healing in this act of deep repentance. A woman of fifty was molested sexually by her father at the age of seven. 'Don't tell Mum', he had said, 'she might be angry.' This poor lady had lived for the last thirty-five or forty years with the guilt both of that occasion, and of what had happened when she was fourteen. When she had asked her father for some money, he had agreed to give her the money on the condition that she let him sleep with her. She had agreed and allowed him to commit incest with her. She came to Audrey and me for ministry, and told us about this experience, and we used what some people have thought was a harsh word. We told her that she had been a prostitute at the age of fourteen. She had slept with a man for the sake of money. We suggested that she asked the Lord's forgiveness for having been a prostitute. This she proceeded to do, and there was a lovely, heartfelt prayer that the Lord would forgive her for this sin and set her free. Then I remember the shout of joy as she said, 'The pain has gone!' We asked her what on earth she was talking about. She explained that for a long time she had had bad rheumatism in her left shoulder and her left arm, but as she received the forgiveness of her sins for that act of prostitution, she received the physical healing. She told us afterwards, that it was our helping her to face up to the fact that she had actually been a prostitute which brought about the release and the forgiveness. Other people who had ministered to her had tried to gloss over the situation by showing her sympathy and saying that it wasn't her fault, and therefore she didn't need to confess it as a sin. Sin has to be faced, as such, and be confessed, before a person can receive God's forgiveness.

That experience was interesting, because it was a complete replay of the incident two thousand years ago, when four friends brought the man who was sick of the palsy (now called Parkinson's disease) to Jesus.[72] As Jesus forgave his sins the man was healed. You will remember that the Pharisees were shocked that a mere man, as they thought, should forgive sins, which was for God alone to do. You will remember Jesus' reply, 'Which is easier, to tell a man that his sins are forgiven, or to tell him to get up and walk?' He turned to the man and told him to get up and walk, which he then promptly did.

Roy is a man in his middle thirties who came to see me. He wanted once again that first, carefree joy which so many people experience in their early days of being Christians. I led him in the prayer of repentance, showing him that of himself there was nothing in him that came up to the Lord's standard, and showing him that he needed to beat his breast and cry out to the Lord from the depths of his heart, saying 'Lord, have mercy upon me a sinner.'

Roy experienced the release and the joy of deep forgiveness, and it was easy to go on from there to recommitment, as he recognised the sheer love of the Lord in having forgiven him for all his sinfulness. It was so easy for him then just to tell the Lord that he wanted to give himself totally to Him, all over again. He told the Lord how sorry he was for the various areas of his life in which, without realising, he had drawn back, and he rededicated himself in every area.

Roy left with a free heart. I told him to concentrate on that act of total commitment to the Lord, and I assured him that before long those first wonderful feelings of freedom and joy would be coming back to him. As he left he said he was already beginning to experience them again.

# 16

# The Language of the Holy Spirit

It was in 1975 that first one of us and then the other received the gift of tongues. Although St Paul refers several times to the gift of 'speaking in other tongues' in his first letter to the church in Corinth, he gives no actual description of what is involved. The language which is given by God seems to be different for each one of us. It seems as if mentally one slips into neutral gear, and allows the words of the Holy Spirit to bubble up from within oneself.

There is, sadly, much controversy about this gift. When I realised I'd received it, I felt I ought to tell my vicar, Bernard, about it. Rather obliquely I raised the subject. But Bernard was no fool. He went straight to the point. 'Has the Lord given you this gift?' he challenged me. I hung my head rather sheepishly, and said, 'Well, actually, Bernard—actually, I think He has.' I always remember Bernard's very wise reply. 'The Lord hasn't given me that gift', he said, 'But I've heard people speaking in tongues, it is very beautiful, and I believe it is of the Lord. But,' and he poked me in my tummy with his finger to stress the point, 'Don't you ever forget, Andy,' he said, 'that love is a thousand times more important than the gift of tongues.' They were wise words. The gift of tongues is not vital. The promise of eternal life does not depend on it. However, it is a practical help.

I notice that those who query the gift of tongues are those who haven't received it, whereas invariably those who have received the gift and use it say what a help it is. I know that for my part I am an ordinary, sinful man, and I need all the help I can get. I find it as hard as the next man to love the Lord, and to worship Him. If the ability to address Him in the language of the Spirit aids my worship then I accept that gift gratefully. All of us have days when God seems a million miles away, and it seems as if we are praying to a blank wall. Often we can come into the sense of His presence by using our imagination. But an even better way, if we have that gift, is to switch over to praying in tongues. Then within a few moments we are aware once again, of the presence of Jesus with us, and we are just pouring out our hearts to Him and telling Him how much we love Him.

Then, too, all of us as Christians are well aware of being led into temptation by Satan. Often, Satan's temptations are very subtle. If, when one realises one is being tempted, one can just switch into tongues, then in Audrey's nice phrase, 'it rolls Satan back'. I remember once we were ministering to a girl who had suffered, and was still suffering, from clinical depression. She rang us up one night, an hour before she was due to come to us for ministry, saying that she was just so sunk in the depths of black despair, that there was no question of her coming to us. Her only thought was to get into bed, pull the bedclothes over her head, and try to sleep, taking a heavy dose of sleeping pills. But we told her that as a Christian she could not give in like this. We told her to pray, non-stop, in tongues from the moment she put down the receiver to the moment she arrived for ministry. She had to come by public transport, and we said that the only exception was when she was actually sitting in the train, when she could, if she preferred, read St John's Gospel. 'But,' we added, 'the moment you get out of that train, back you go to praying in tongues.' An hour later she arrived. There is no doubt that all Christians suffer temptation, perhaps in varying intensity, and the gift of tongues is a real help in combating this.

It is also a help in other ways. Sophie and her husband were having real difficulties in their marriage. After some twenty years of marriage he had slipped, and, although his repentance was immediate and sincere, she just couldn't forgive him. He longed to forget the whole wretched incident, but she kept on bringing it up again and again. This led to a continuing series of rows which were getting more and more intense, and they were even thinking of separation. We told her that, for the sake of her husband—and she loved him deeply—she had simply got to forgive him. But on this occasion there was no power in our ministry. She just wasn't able to carry out what we said. The healing of their marriage only came when one of the elders in their church advised her to pray a lot in tongues. Only then was she able to forgive.

I think, too, of A. A is seventy and has a severe pain in her lower stomach, which the doctors say they can't cure. Somehow she tries to cope with the pain, for she refuses to take lots of painkillers. She telephoned early one morning as the pain was so intense. She had received the gift of tongues some three weeks earlier, but hadn't used it. I said to her: 'Pray in tongues as soon as you feel the pain and, if necessary, go on non-stop.' I asked her on the telephone, later in the day, how she had got on. 'Marvellous,' was her reply. She added, however, that the pain had returned in the evening—when I gathered she had stopped praying in tongues.

But is that gift of tongues for all of us? Surely Paul makes it clear that each of the nine gifts of the Spirit which he enumerates[73] is for one person or another, and it is not for us to believe that all of them are for all of us?

Yet two chapters later he wrote: 'I would like every one of you to speak in tongues.'[74] He also affirmed that he 'who speaks in tongues edifies himself'[75] and he extols the value of praying in tongues in one's own private prayers. (He wrote: 'I thank God that I speak in tongues more than all of you.'[76] He continues: 'But in the church . . .' from which it seems clear that the earlier words refer to private prayer.)[77]

Although 1 Corinthians 12 is not particularly clear on this point, that chapter seems to be a description of a group of Christians meeting together for praise and worship. Taken in that context, the chapter is readily understandable. In such a meeting, it is indeed true that one or two people may be given a message in tongues; one or two may be given an interpretation;

a prophecy may be given to someone else; someone may be given a gift of faith for a specific need; others will exercise different gifts of healing; someone will be given a gift of performing a miracle on that occasion, and so on, through the nine gifts of the Spirit which St Paul lists.

Judging by sheer experience, the Lord is pouring out the gift of tongues everywhere today. I don't know how many hundreds of people Audrey and I have prayed for to receive that gift—and we make a rule not to pray for people to receive that gift unless they have first asked for it. But the number of occasions on which we have prayed for people to receive that gift, and they have not received it, then and there, are very few.

I remember the occasion when a great friend of ours, Jackie Pullinger, was ministering in our village church at home. She gave a talk, and then said that if anyone was interested in receiving this gift, would they please remain behind. After the service was over, half a dozen young people gathered in the front pew. While Jackie ministered to them, I was praying quietly in the background. Then she came to the man at the end. Jackie turned to me and said, 'Andy, you go over and pray with him.' Now it happens that I am slightly deaf, and I hadn't heard the man say that he would prefer to receive the gift of tongues, alone, at home that evening. So, unaware of this, I prayed that the Lord would give him the gift of tongues. He received it there and then. I learnt subsequently, that he met another friend of mine in London, the following day. He told him the story, and both of them joined together in saying, 'Thank God for Andy's deafness!'

The first time Audrey and I ever ministered to anyone who was seeking this gift, was the first time we met Jackie. This was when Charlie was still at Cambridge, and as we were the only parents present, we were given the job of taking this young missionary from Hong Kong out to lunch. We entertained her and found her fascinating; later we joined about a hundred and twenty undergraduates, and all listened spellbound while she talked for an hour and three-quarters about her experiences ministering to drug addicts in downtown

Hong Kong. She then said that the meeting was over, and everyone could go, but if anyone was seeking the gift of tongues, would they stay behind. It seemed nobody moved. In the event, I believe about forty people left, but eighty remained, far too many for Jackie herself to pray with, individually. I remember our feeling of horror as she turned to us and said, 'Well, get on. Go and pray for them to receive.' We had never prayed for anyone to receive the gift of tongues before, and we hesitated. 'That's all right,' Jackie reassured us, 'it'll be the Lord who gives them the gift, not you.' There was nothing for it and, with one after another, we prayed for the undergraduates to receive the gift of tongues. As so often happens in our lives, when the Lord throws us in at the deep end, and we are prepared to step out and make fools of ourselves for Him, He honours us; it was a great excitement as we prayed for these undergraduates and one after the other they started quietly bubbling forth in the language of the Holy Spirit which He had given them. I remember two strapping rowing men, who we came to. The first one said that he had already been given the gift of tongues, but only a couple of words, so we told him we weren't going to waste time with him. His friend hadn't received the gift at all. So we told the first that he should lay hands on his friend, along with us, and we would all pray for the friend to receive this gift. As the friend received, so the first one was released into a fluent flow of the language of the Holy Spirit, and we left these two grown men hugging each other in joy at the gift the Lord had given them.

What is abundantly clear is that there is one person who has a vested interest, either in our not receiving the gift of tongues, or, if he fails in that respect, in our not using it. I refer, of course, to Satan. Some people have difficulty in accepting the fact of there being an embodiment of evil, such as we call Satan, or the devil. Obviously, no one now believes in a goat-like figure with a tail, two horns and a pitchfork in his hand. But if the power of goodness and of love is headed up by a Person, it seems to me to be logical to think in terms of the powers of darkness and of evil, similarly being headed up by a person. Consequently, I have no difficulty, myself, in accepting the existence of the devil, or Satan—call him what you will.

The devil has a vested interest in preventing the use of tongues, as it is a powerful weapon against him, in the mouth of the Christian. When people are seeking this gift, we warn them that Satan will very likely try and tell them that they are not good enough to receive it; it is all very well for other people to receive it, but why should the Lord give it to people like them? Satan manages, through his lies, to put on so many of us an unhealthy feeling of our own unworthiness. Then, when they receive the gift of tongues, Satan will try and tell them that they are making it up, and that it is just gibberish.

Again, we remind people not to look for any dramatic manifestations of the Holy Spirit. Indeed the whole experience of receiving the gift of tongues may well seem so 'unspiritual' that they will wonder if it can be genuine!

When someone seeks to receive this gift, we explain that frequently, in the stories of the healing miracles in the Gospels, Jesus required the person to do something specific themselves. There was the occasion in Luke's Gospel, when Jesus healed the ten lepers. He didn't simply look at them, have pity on them, and say, 'Be healed.' He told them to go and show themselves to the priest, as laid down in the law of Moses, to show that they had been healed.[78] It is clear from careful reading of Luke's account, that as they set off, shambling down the road to where the priest lived, they had not, at that stage, been healed. Luke tells us that, as they went, they were healed. They had to set out and do something in their own strength first, and then the miracle followed.

We see the same principle with the woman with the issue of blood. Women were looked down on in Jesus' day. There was a great crowd of people thronging around Jesus; natives in a primitive country have no inhibitions about pressing close against one another. It must have been a sheer physical struggle for that woman to burrow through, between the bodies of all those men, and to get close enough to Him to be

177

able to touch the hem of His garment. However, she made the effort, and Jesus commended her, saying that her faith had healed her.[79]

Again there is the story of when Jesus appeared, walking on the water. Peter called out to Him and Jesus replied, 'Come'.[80] Now the odds are that Peter was probably sitting in the bottom of the boat. It was not as if two great celestial hands came and scooped him up bodily, lifting him out of the boat and setting him on the solid surface of the water. No; Peter had to move, first, in his own strength. He had himself to get up from where he was sitting, he had to swing first one leg over the side of the boat, and then the other, and he had to slide off the edge of the boat on to the water. It was only then, after he had made the effort, that the miracle happened.

Thus, in the same way, as we seek the gift of tongues, it is no use our just sitting there, with our mouth open, waiting for some miraculous force to start moving our tongue and our lips. We need deliberately to make some sounds—any sounds except English words. Then the miracle follows. Somehow the sounds which come are the beginnings of the language of the Holy Spirit.

Sometimes the Lord only gives us a few words. My sister was literally only given one phrase in tongues for about six months. But she persevered, finding this phrase useful as she worshipped the Lord each day, and after six months, the Lord had grown it into a lovely language of the Holy Spirit.

Quite often, as we start to pray in tongues, it seems that the sounds are childish and babbling. In a way this may be so. When a young couple have their first baby, one day when father comes back from work, the mother will not say proudly to him, 'Baby has just started speaking perfect English.' She will say, 'Baby said "Dada" for the first time today!' I think very often that the Lord just gives us the beginning of the language of the Holy Spirit, and then, as we practise that language faithfully, so He grows it into a flowing, melodious language of tongues. It took me about two years to become fluent in my language. But some people, like Audrey, are fluent straight away.

I remember leading a girl to the Lord, and then praying for her to receive the gift of tongues. There was a long pause. Then suddenly she started bubbling forth in tongues. Subsequently, she told me that it had been exactly as I had warned her. As I prayed for her to receive the gift of tongues, the thought came firmly into her mind, 'This is all a lot of rubbish; nothing whatsoever is going to happen.' So long as she harboured that thought, nothing happened. Then she remembered my warning her that Satan would try and stop her receiving. So she rebuked him, and she told me, 'As I rebuked him, and told him to get lost, the language suddenly started to flow, and I was able to praise the Lord in tongues.'

Sometimes people pray in tongues in a known language, and sometimes not. I think St Paul must have had this in mind when he wrote that lovely hymn of love, which we know as 1 Corinthians chapter 13. At the beginning of that chapter, he refers to speaking 'with the tongues of men and of angels', and I think he had in mind that sometimes the gift of tongues is an earthly language, and sometimes, perhaps, a language of angels. We remember once being at a prayer meeting with Jackie Pullinger when a girl of nineteen who worked in the Army and Navy Stores in our local town at home, confessed that she sometimes used words that she didn't know, but she had real doubts as to whether it was the gift of tongues. Jackie told her to come next door, and to pray with her, speaking these funny words. She told us afterwards that, after hearing the girl using these words, she had asked her whether anyone had ever taught her Latin or Italian. The girl said she had never learnt either language. 'Well', Jackie said, 'as you prayed in tongues, as you were undoubtedly doing then, you were praising the Lord quite beautifully in fluent Italian.'

There is another nice story, which we heard from a friend who worships regularly at Chard. A Frenchman came to a service, and the woman next to him was given a message in tongues. She spoke in French with a Parisian accent. The man knew in his heart, as soon as he heard the words in his own language, that the Lord was speaking directly to him.

He missed the woman, after the service, but insisted on telephoning her to thank her for the message she had given him. We know her well and she told him that never in her life had she learnt a word of French. The gift of tongues may indeed be a human language. I have no knowledge of what mine is, and quite frankly, I don't mind. All that matters to me is that I know, beyond doubt, that it is of the Lord.

Some people are frightened of the gift of tongues, because they believe it is emotional, and that one is out of control. It is simply not true that one is out of control when one prays in tongues. If the language is genuinely from the Holy Spirit, it is completely under one's control. One can start it at will. One can stop it at will. One can turn up the volume, as it were, and one can turn down the volume. But what one cannot do, is to change the words as they come. One needs to follow where the Holy Spirit is leading, and let the words come. Furthermore, we find it is often helpful to tell people not to listen to what they are saying. So long as you keep your eyes on the Lord, and think in terms of worshipping Him, and of using these strange sounds to worship Him better, then they flow gently and smoothly. But, if you take your eyes off the Lord and start listening to what you are saying, often the words dry up, for you're not meant to be doing that. It is not a gift which is given to us for curiosity, it is a practical aid to worship, to ministry and to Christian living. Always, when people receive it, it seems to bring them joy. We have never known anybody who wasn't thrilled when they were given that gift, even if it was only a few words. It seems, quite apart from anything else, to be a lovely, tangible evidence of the love of Jesus for them.

The gift of tongues is meant to be used. Quite often, people come to us who say that at one time they talked in tongues, but they say, 'I wasn't sure if it was genuine; perhaps I was fooling myself, and so I didn't use it.' It only takes a few minutes prayer to get them going again. But this does show how Satan will do anything he can to stop us using that language of spiritual power. We do well to pray in tongues frequently throughout the day; I often pray in tongues if I am driving the car, and no one is with me.

While I was still working in the City, when I had had a heavy day, with perhaps a whole series of board meetings and interviews, and perhaps I came back for a quick wash and change, before going out to a business dinner, I was often quite tired, and feeling in need of a pick-me-up. I know of nothing more restful, after a heavy day, than to lie for ten minutes in a hot bath, praying the while in tongues. Often in the City, as I went from one meeting to another, I would pray in tongues on the way—under my breath, but nonetheless, in tongues.

I remember, too, an occasion when I had to drive from our home, in Surrey, up to Manchester. It was a five-hour drive. I was driving alone, and I had always recognised that one of my weaknesses was that I was unable to drive more than about an hour and a half before getting a severe pain in my neck and shoulders. There was no option on this occasion, I had to do it, but I was dreading the journey; I thought I would have to stop for several rests. However, it occurred to me to pray in tongues. I think I prayed or sang in tongues for almost the whole way. I didn't stop the car, other than to fill up with petrol, and I realised when I arrived, that I felt as fresh as a daisy. Furthermore, it wasn't as though the Lord used that time of praying in tongues merely to help me through a long, solo drive. It wasn't till some months later that I realised He had used that occasion to heal me, and never again have I been bothered about having to do a long drive.

Jackie Pullinger, in her book, *Chasing the Dragon*, recounts how, while working with opium and heroin addicts in the brothel area of Hong Kong, she has found that as she prays for them to be baptised in the Holy Spirit, and to receive the gift of tongues, they are able to come off drug addiction without any pain. I think most of us know the American expression, coming off drugs 'cold turkey'. If a person comes off hard drugs, without any medication, there is a period lasting three days of really intense pain, and during which the skin goes pimply—hence the expression 'cold turkey'. But Jackie has told us that if the drug addict has received the gift of tongues, as soon as the appalling stomach cramp comes on, he or she has only to switch over to praying in tongues, and the pain goes.

Ever since it dawned on me that I really had a Heavenly Father who delights to give His children good things, my response has been: 'Thank you, Lord, and if it's really going to give you pleasure, I'd love to have the lot, please!' There are other gifts of the Holy Spirit which are obviously good, and I continue to wait on Him to give me just as many of the gifts of the Holy Spirit, as He will. Sometimes people come to us and say that they mustn't be greedy. I think all of us need to be greedy for all the blessings and the gifts which the Lord longs to give us; indeed St Paul tells us to seek the gifts of His Spirit. After all, if we don't seek them, there is a sense in which we are turning our back on them; it always seems to us rather ungrateful not to be enthusiastic about some gift which a loving Father is longing to give us.

Jesus foresaw that, after His ascension, when the disciples came to be baptised in the Holy Spirit and to receive the gift of speaking in tongues, they would receive a new power in their ministry. This is something which I don't think has yet come to be sufficiently emphasised in the current time of renewal in the churches. We hear a lot—and rightly—about the need for Christians to be filled with the Holy Spirit. But often, even so, churches still seem to be without real spiritual power. We need not only a release of the Holy Spirit within us, but a release of His power. After all, no one we may minister to is really set free, changed or healed without some release of spiritual power. Having been filled with His Holy Spirit, we need to press on, and appropriate more and more of the power of the Holy Spirit.

St Luke, in his Gospel, seems to point to there having been perhaps two phases with Jesus. He records that Jesus, after His baptism, was 'full of the Holy Spirit'.[81] Then, thirteen verses later, he says He went up into Galilee 'in the *power* of the Spirit'.[82] The intervening verses tell of Jesus' suffering and His battle with Satan, when He was tempted in the wilderness. Doctors tell us that it is after some forty days of

182

fasting that the body fat has been used up, and the really acute hunger sets in. Jesus vanquished Satan during that time of suffering and temptation, and the power of the Holy Spirit was further released in Him.

Let us remember that if we, too, seem to go through a particularly severe time of spiritual testing, after we have been filled with the Holy Spirit, it may be the prelude to the Lord releasing in us more of the power of His Spirit.

Now where does this power derive from? Who do we pray to? Do we pray to Jesus? Or do we pray to God? I know lovely Christians who pray to their Heavenly Father, and I'm certain they're right. Jesus Himself, told us when we pray, to say, 'Our Father'.[83] Yet, I also know many Christians who pray to Jesus, and I'm certain that they, too, are right. After all Jesus said 'I and the Father are one',[84] and as we read St John's Gospel, in particular, it is very clear that God revealed Himself in the person of Jesus.

The words at the end of St Matthew's Gospel are relevant. Before His ascension into Heaven, Jesus told His disciples, 'All authority in heaven and on earth has been given to me',[85] and if one is praying the prayer of command, perhaps in deliverance, and sometimes in healing, it is necessary to use the name and authority of Jesus. The ultimate power is in the name of Jesus. When Peter and John saw the lame man at the gate of the Temple, Peter said, 'In the name of Jesus Christ of Nazareth, walk.'[86] Time and again, in the book of Acts, it is the name of Jesus which those early disciples used as they prayed in power.

For a long time I was puzzled that there didn't seem to be the same power in the name of God. Then I learnt that 'God' is not in fact a proper noun. 'God' is only a noun, it is not the personal name of God; and we no longer know the personal name of God. He revealed His personal name in the Old Testament times to the Jews, but the Jews had no vowels in their writing. They only had consonants. Out of those consonants we have derived the names Jahweh and Jehovah. But at best, those are only guesses as to what the personal name of God is. From about the year 300 BC, the Jews never dared to use the personal name of God, because they stood in such awe of the power there was in that name, and they were afraid of using it improperly and blasphemously. The name was still remembered, however, in the time of Jesus, but then, when Jerusalem was destroyed by the Romans, in AD 70, it was lost.

I've sometimes wondered why God did not choose again to reveal His own personal name, but the answer seems clear. God sent His only begotten Son, Jesus, to live for us, to die for us, and to rise again for us, and as Jesus told His disciples, He put all authority in Heaven and Earth into His hands. We know the personal name of the Son of God, namely Jesus, and having His Name, there was, I believe, no longer the need to know the personal name of God. Power is in the name of Jesus.

# 17

# And the Future?

Many of the social reformers of past years would rejoice at what has now been achieved in their field. The long hours of drudgery in factories have been stopped by legislation. The acute poverty and hunger of pre-war years are no more. The days when a child might fall sick and yet medical help would be denied him for lack of money, are gone. The welfare state provides a safety net beyond which we cannot fall. Free medical help is available; free education is on hand, and for almost everyone in the population there is the entertainment of a television set.

Yet in many ways, we are as far as ever from the heaven on earth which the social reformers would have foreseen with the material blessings which we have today. Although it is a truism that we live in a materialistic age, there is a spiritual hunger. Mental sickness and, in particular, depression are on the increase. Half the beds in the National Health Service hospitals are for patients suffering from mental illness. In the search for stability, men and girls regularly live together before marriage, then stability escapes them and breakdowns in marriage continue to increase. As a consequence, both men and women are damaged emotionally, whilst the damage to the children whose parents have split up is often greater. The use of hard drugs is on the increase, whilst countless people are only able to face life with regular doses of tranquillisers.

Meanwhile, if we look below the surface, I think in many ways we are sitting on a time bomb. Unemployment in this country, as in most industrialised countries of the West, is at a high level. Trouble has broken out in inner city areas, stemming largely from the frustration of young people who, after a period of compulsory education, are now thrown out into a world in which there seems no prospect of a worthwhile job. As the Victorians used to say, Satan finds work for idle hands to do, and this is equally true whether those hands are idle through their own volition or through force of circumstances. I believe in the years to come we are likely to see more inner city disturbances.

Internationally, it is broadly true that an uneasy peace has been sustained between the world powers because the United States has had the preponderance of power, and the United States wants peace. The other two great superpowers, Russia and China, are however not democracies but dictatorships. There is always the risk that a new group of men will come to power in one country or the other who feel they are now strong enough to achieve their will by force.

Meanwhile, nuclear energy becomes more freely available to the lesser powers, with the danger of one or other of their regimes exploding a nuclear bomb and setting off an international conflagration. After all, it was only the murder of an Archduke in some small town in the Balkans, which set off the horror and bloodshed of the First World War.

Then there is the problem of the world's resources. The resources which are needed to maintain an industrialised civilisation are by no means unlimited. Well within the lifetimes of many of us who live today, the world will begin to run out of those resources which seem to be vital if we are to maintain our industrialised society. Even more important than industrial raw materials is food, and the prospect of eliminating hunger in the world is as far off as ever. If our industrialised society should break down, whether through lack of resources, through internal unrest, or through international action, the outlook would be bleak indeed. Two or three generations ago, many of our forebears lived on the land, and if necessary could have sustained themselves from the land which they themselves tilled. Indeed, at the beginning of the century in this country, the main occupation for men was in agriculture. But now we have become more 'civilised'. If there was a breakdown of the highly complicated society in which we live today, mass starvation would follow, and this in turn would be accompanied by a total breakdown of law and order.

We may prefer not to think of these things. We may prefer to be like the proverbial ostrich, and hide our heads in the sand. Certainly, it does no good to let the fear of such matters dominate our lives. But for a responsible, thinking person, the question must arise: what can I do?

It seems to us that there can, indeed, only be one answer. That is, to confess not only our own sinfulness, but the sinfulness and folly of our generation, to turn back to the Lord[87] and seek to love Him with all our heart and soul and strength and mind.[88] As we love Him, we can rest in His peace, and He can then work through us; we can achieve so much more in this strength than on our own.

Jesus promised: 'I will never turn away anyone who comes to me.'[89]

Mankind has proved incapable of solving the problems of this world. Only God can solve them.

# Living in Victory

1. It is easy to say the words of a confession of sin. It is less easy to mean them from the heart. What matters, though, is if you *want* to mean them from the heart. In that case, our Lord accepts the words as being genuine and sincere. You need to confess *all* your sins, known or unknown, remembered or forgotten.

   Then, when you have prayed through the prayer of repentance, acknowledge that Jesus, in His love for you, has completely forgiven you; that He has accepted you and that He has washed you clean with His blood. Thank Him in faith that all this is, in fact, true.

2. Remember that the feeling of guilt is almost always the voice of Satan. If the Lord wants us to drop some part of our life which is offensive to Him, and saddens Him, He speaks with the still small voice of calm knowledge—though a voice which can at times be very firm. But the Lord doesn't talk with the nagging, accusing voice of guilt.

3. Satan often works through echoes. If we are among steep hills, it often happens that if we shout there is an echo. From the echo, it sounds as if a real person is calling to us, but we know that isn't true. We know it is only an echo.

   We may, for example, ask the Lord to heal us, say, of fear. Because the Lord is always faithful, He answers that prayer and takes away the fear.

   But Satan doesn't want us to be free from the fear. He, therefore, tries to make us believe that we are still subject to the fear, and he will project on to us a feeling of fear.

When this happens, we need to recognise that the feeling of fear is as much an illusion as the sound of a real voice when we hear an echo. As we recognise this, it gives us courage to rebuke Satan and tell him in the name of Jesus, and by the power of His blood, to stop telling us lies. Then we thank Jesus, in faith, for taking away the fear.

4. If you are feeling self-conscious, you are really listening to the voice of Satan saying that you know you're no good.

This is Satan lying. You were created in the image of God. Jesus died that you might be set free. No-one has any right to think of you as being worthless. If they do, they are criticising God's handiwork, and/or they are saying that Jesus left His work unfinished on Calvary.

If you are alone a lot, remember that the best cure for loneliness is to pray for other people.

5. Remember that your instructions from the Lord are that you must love Him with all your heart and soul and mind and strength, and your neighbour as yourself. This is not friendly advice, nor even loving counsel. These are instructions which you are expected to obey.

Remember that one day will be your last day in this world. When you get up each day, reflect that it could always be your last day. You might find yourself face to face with God before the evening. This helps one to concentrate on doing His will each day.

Try to live through the day remembering—something which is actually true of course—that you are in His presence. Keep asking yourself what you can do which will bring Him joy and will glorify Him. Try and lead yourself so that you live for Him, giving yourself to Him and enjoying doing what will give Him joy.

6. You love the Lord—what can you be doing right now to make Him feel pleased with you and proud of you?

You may know, perhaps, what the answer is. You may know what you ought to be doing. Remember, then, that you must make the first step; then, after you have made that first step, a miracle will happen and you will find that Jesus is supporting you with His strength.

When the Lord told Peter to walk on the water, Peter got up from his seat in the boat in his own strength and trusting the Lord that He would then do a miracle. Peter stepped out of the boat in his own strength and then the miracle happened and the water supported him.

When Jesus wanted to heal the ten lepers, He told them to show themselves to the priest. They started down the road to where the priest lived, in their own strength, and using their own wills. It was only then that the miracle happened and they were healed.

Perhaps your will has become weak from lack of use. After all, if we are in bed for a fortnight with flu, our legs will have become weak from the lack of use. We don't then sit back and say, 'I can't walk because my legs are so weak'; instead we take a few steps the first day, and then a few more, and gradually the strength returns to our legs.

If your will has become weak because you haven't used it, start using it again gradually, and increasingly, in just the same way.

7. You may find that you are depressed and you feel you don't have it in you to pray to God and to praise Him. You may feel that, under these circumstances, it would be hypocritical. Don't let that worry you. Be obedient to God by reading His Word and speaking to Him with your mouth. If the desire to praise Him is there, whether you feel like it or not, if you praise Him obediently with your lips the feelings will follow afterwards.

Similarly, claim the Bible passages about victory out aloud. Claim them as applying to you.

8. Ask yourself the following questions and don't just give quick answers. Reflect on each one to see whether the answer you give is something you really believe with your own heart.
    (a)  Do you believe in Jesus?
    (b)  Do you believe that He is a real person?
    (c)  Do you believe that He is here with you now?
    (d)  Do you believe He loves you?
    (e)  Do you believe He has heard your request?
    (f)  Do you believe He is able to help you and heal you?

(g) Do you believe He wants to?

(h) Do you believe He is going to?—now?

Step out in faith and thank Him that He has heard your prayer, and that He has now got the matter in hand and is acting on it. There is power in the prayer of thanks, because you can't thank Him for something and still entertain doubts. As you thank Him you quell the voice of doubt, and your faith is actually strengthened.

9. If we have a problem, depression for example, it is very easy to let that problem become central in our lives. This is what Satan wants, as we then take our eyes off Jesus. It is as if we were out walking in hilly country and, coming around a corner, we find a great rock blocking our path and we just stand looking at it.

Instead, take your eyes deliberately off the problem—walk round the rock—and look again at Jesus. Give yourself afresh to Jesus in love and thank Him that you are His and He is leading you.

If you are seeking physical healing, picture your body whole and as if it has already been healed. Then turn your mind to Jesus, thank Him that His healing power is already working in your body. Keep on picturing Him bringing about your complete healing.

Perhaps you are feeling depressed. You have no energy and you have a low opinion of yourself. Then picture yourself as Jesus wants you to be and, indeed, as He longs to transform you. See yourself relaxed; at peace; rejoicing in the love of Jesus your Lord; and free to go out with energy and joy to bring His love and His healing to those around you. Thank Him that He is already bringing this 'you' into being.

10. Many of us remember how, as a very small child, when we were frightened or bewildered, we ran to some grown-up we trusted. We reached up to hold their hand—and we felt safe once again.

Do the same with Jesus. All of us are still children in our hearts. If you are frightened or bewildered, reach up and, in your mind, take hold of His hand and allow yourself to feel the comfort and security He longs to give you.

11. Job said: 'What I feared has come upon me.' If we allow ourselves to be afraid that something which isn't of the Lord is going to happen to us, it probably will. That fear is of Satan. Ask the Lord to protect you from that happening and then keep on thanking Him in faith that He has heard that prayer and He has now got the situation in hand, and you can trust Him to look after you.

Each time you give in to Satan, it strengthens his grip on you. Each time you resist his attack, it weakens him for the next time.

Remember that faith works in reverse too. If you allow yourself to say 'I can't' you are actually exercising faith that you won't be able to do what you had in mind. And then you *won't* be able to do it.

Ask the Lord to help you to do it and then keep thanking Him that He, through His power, is enabling you to do it.

The best way to overcome fear is to go out, without hesitating, and *do* what you are afraid of. Then you'll find that it isn't really as bad as you thought it was going to be.

12. Finally, think of this: If you were walking along the pavement carrying several heavy suitcases, and a friend rushed up to you offering to help carry them, suppose you looked straight through him, ignored him, and went on carrying the suitcases, wouldn't your friend feel hurt and rejected?

We have a loving heavenly Father who is infinite compassion and who is always longing to help us in His own perfect way. Thank Him for His help and accept it. Don't go struggling in your own strength and ignore Him.

Rev Andy Arbuthnot,
Missioner,
LONDON HEALING MISSION
20 DAWSON PLACE
LONDON W2 4TL
Tel: 01 229 3641